Six Plays

Six Plays

Archibald MacLeish

Houghton Mifflin Company
Boston 1980

Copyright © 1980 by Archibald MacLeish
Foreword copyright © 1980 by Houghton Mifflin Company

Library of Congress Cataloging in Publication Data
MacLeish, Archibald,   date
  Six plays.

  CONTENTS: Nobodaddy. — Panic. — The fall of the
city. — [etc.]
  I. Title.
PS3525.A27S5   812'.52   80–92
ISBN 0–395–28419–8

Printed in the United States of America

V 10 9 8 7 6 5 4 3 2 1

The plays have been published previously as follows: *Nobodaddy*, by Dunster
House; *Fall of the City*, by Farrar and Rinehart; *Air Raid*, by Harcourt Brace;
Panic and *The Trojan Horse*, by Houghton Mifflin; *This Music Crept by Me
upon the Waters*, by Harvard University Press.

Contents

FOREWORD · ix

NOBODADDY · 1

PANIC · 31

THE FALL OF THE CITY · 65

AIR RAID · 95

THE TROJAN HORSE · 125

THIS MUSIC CREPT BY ME UPON THE WATERS · 167

Foreword: A Poet's Task

At the center of Archibald MacLeish's plays is an exploration of the nature of man — man both distinguished by his own human nature and in the company of his fellows. Writing through a half century in which the idea of man has been tried by dictatorship, depression, fascism, communism, McCarthyism, and even the recent attempt at an imperial presidency, MacLeish has remained constant in his defense of man's nobility and of the importance of a political and social structure that will allow an individual to exercise those qualities that make him human. The plays in this volume are all distinguished examples of the poet's attempt to discover this human spirit and to define those changes that have come upon it in our own time.

MacLeish's own exploration of the fundamentals of the human condition rose from the profound sense of doubt that typified the years before, during, and after the First World War. His Scots father had once been destined for the Kirk. His Connecticut Yankee mother was the daughter of a Congregational minister. In early years he was surrounded by highly educated adults and guided by a way of life that included daily family prayers, Sunday service at the Baptist church and, at twelve, a baptism that he felt at the time to be a "religious experience." But by the time MacLeish arrived at Yale (1911) his faith had been bedeviled by the doubts he later realized held his whole generation. And, by 1918, he had begun to sense that a world had ended with the "unspeakable disaster" of the First World War.

> It was not easy for us — not easy even for a man as perceptive as Mr. Wilson — to accept the fact that the world was no longer there. But Eliot as poet realized it — and created (his duty as poet) the form in which it could be realized by others. Pound realized it — *in* his poem. Dos Passos found fictions which would realize it. And the realization was the age. It was not the Lost Generation which was lost: It was the world out of which that generation came. And it was not a generation of expatriates who found themselves in Paris in those years but a generation whose *patria,* wherever it may once have been, was now no longer waiting for them anywhere.
>
> ("Expatriates in Paris" in *Riders on the Earth*)

Committed to the art of poetry, MacLeish was faced with the profoundly personal need to understand his experience of the world, and a commitment to the task of making sense of that experience. It was this need for a sense of understanding — for himself, for his contemporaries, for the sake of his time and its belief in man — that led him to the stage and to his first verse play, *Nobodaddy* (1926), with its examination of "the fundamentals of the human condition — the mystery of human consciousness in a universe without consciousness — the great myth of that mystery, the story of Eden."

In his original foreword to *Nobodaddy,* MacLeish explained that the play — whatever other meanings it might hold — explores the beginnings of human consciousness. But it is also

x

interesting to view *Nobodaddy's* struggle for human value against the background of its author's personal search for direction during the period immediately prior to his writing of the play. In another essay in *Riders on the Earth* MacLeish described a period in 1923, five years after his war experience and four years after Harvard Law School, when he was employed by a prestigious Boston law firm. Working to support his wife and two children, he could find time for his own writing only on rare weekend hours.

> I was simply a young man, not so young as I had been once, trying to teach myself to write better than I had written: a young man who had had a volume of verses published when he went off to the wars, and now had another ready, and a publisher willing, but who knew, although he couldn't have told you why, that something had gone wrong. I was writing, yes, but out of the margins of my life, and the work showed it: lines like letters from a brief vacation in another country. And though I had solved, as I thought, the problem of supporting a family and writing verse, I did not *feel* I had solved anything. If I had, why should I wake at morning with that sense of *owing?* Owing what? To whom?
>
> ("Autobiographical Information" in *Riders on the Earth*)

The resolution of this problem came to him "on a clear, cold, winter evening in February." Lured from his customary subway ride from State Street to Cambridge by a new moon, MacLeish began the two-hour walk home.

> I was opposite Eliot House when the moon went down. So that was what I'd done . . . had *not* done. I had prepared, provided, made arrangements for a time to come, for work to come, for art to come. There is no art to come: there's only art — the need, the now, the presence, the necessity . . . the sun.

It was the art I owed.

I started up the little path beside the river. Ran. Turned off beyond the Landing. One light in the little house. "Where were you? I've been telephoning . . ." "I know. I have to talk to you. I don't want anything to eat . . ." We talked all night or most of it. She seemed to know what I would say before I'd said it. We made our plans, rose early . . . and the ironies began.

It was not yet nine when I got to the office. I asked to see the senior partner whom I had worked with, loved; was told that he was waiting for me. I walked in. The members of the firm were standing round the room. They had just elected me to partnership . . .

That winter evening provides interesting background for *Nobodaddy*, a play about man striving to become the center of his universe. MacLeish would affirm a few years later that the poet's role was "the restoration of man to his position of dignity and responsibility at the center of his world." In his wintry walk across Boston MacLeish had found the strength necessary to sever (in Cain's words) the thick vein "that knots me to the body of the earth," and to assume the vocation that has been the center of his life's work. Thus *Nobodaddy*, the story of man attempting to make sense of the chaos of life, can also be read as the *Apologia* for its creator's personal decision.

The same question of man's nature and value is explored from a very different perspective in MacLeish's next play, *Panic* (1935). In America a tension was developing between the prophecy of capitalism's collapse and the collapse itself. The prophecy was the Marxist conception of economic necessity, the dialectical inevitability that foretold the collapse of human societies founded on freedom of human choice. The collapse itself involved the vast glacial spread, the inexorable advance of that failure of human enterprise in country after country, which became known as the Great Depression — the paralysis of human mind and human will and apparently of human destiny.

The editorial offices of both the *New Theatre* and the *Daily Worker* were not entirely happy with *Panic*. Michael Gold, the communist writer, had written a review of MacLeish's *Frescoes for Mr. Rockefeller's City* in 1933 entitled "Out of the Fascist Unconscious." "Hitlers' program," he warned, "somewhat veiled in cauls and mysteries of the poetic womb, may also be discerned in these latest verses of Archibald MacLeish." MacLeish, from Gold's viewpoint, was unable to see that to find "the true home of the American tradition" one should turn to the left rather than the right. *Panic*, at first glance, seemed to show that its author had harkened to Gold's view that "this land is great because it was founded on a democratic revolution." Thus, the *Daily Worker* pronounced MacLeish a convert, an "outstanding" American poet who had written a play that "in addition to its remarkable artistic achievement, represents the radical workers as the force that will build a new world." However, *Panic* had not spelled out this ideological conversion as clearly as the editors would have liked. Therefore the newspaper announced that it would sponsor a special performance, to be followed by a critical symposium on the play with Stanley Burnshaw of the *New Masses*, John Howard Lawson for the New Theatre League, V. J. Jerome of *The Communist*, and MacLeish.

This symposium, as MacLeish's new preface relates with more lightness than he probably felt at the time, proved only that the playwright had not, nor would ever, accept Marxist ideology. MacLeish had earlier made this position perfectly clear in a series of articles on the relationship between art and ideology in *The Saturday Review* written during his years as an editor of *Fortune*. There he stated that the panic of Wall Street had been a "panic of intelligence." And he had pointed out that while *as artist* he was "perfectly unconcerned with the name by which the state is to be described, whether capitalistic, or socialistic, or communistic, or Fascist" he believed that "only under capitalism, of all existing alternatives" have artists any real hope of intellectual freedom. MacLeish saw both the Depression and McGafferty's collapse as failures, not of economic freedom, but of man's ability to imagine and pursue the spiritual ideals of democracy with strength and courage.

As MacLeish moved into the last half of the thirties, he returned more and more often to the need for the artist to speak (as he had done in *Panic*) with a public voice.

> In support of fascism, when the time comes, there will be enlisted all the forces which fascism can buy — the press, the movies, the commercial theatre. They will be lined up as they were lined up during the war. Their power will be overwhelming. Against them will stand the artists whom money cannot buy. And yet, and despite the discrepancy in numbers, in wealth, in everything else which creates discrepancies, the conflict will not be unequal. No power on earth can out-persuade the great and greatly felt work of art when its purpose is clear and its creator confident.
>
> ("Question of Audience" in A *Time to Speak*)

The Fall of the City (1937) and *Air Raid* (1938) are further illustrations of the poet's task. And as he became more involved with Roosevelt's administration, MacLeish returned to this theme of the artist's role with increasing frequency. The problems of Depression at home, and fascism abroad exemplified a failure of desire, a failure of imagination. And it was the role of the poet to imagine and create "the world that men can wish to live in and make true." The failure of the spirit, he wrote in 1938,

> . . . is a failure from which only poetry can deliver us. In this incapacity of the people to imagine, this impotence of

the people to imagine and believe, only poetry can be of service. For only poetry, of all those proud and clumsy instruments by which men explore this planet and themselves, *creates the thing it sees*. Only poetry, exploring the spirit of man, is capable of creating in a breathful of words the common good men have become incapable of imagining for themselves.

("In Challenge, Not Defense" in A *Time to Speak*)

A few months later, MacLeish published "Public Speech and Private Speech in Poetry," an essay that explored the importance of Yeats, Eliot, and Pound on the similar basis of poetry's return to the "actual streets and doors and houses of our world." The strength of Yeats' later poetry, MacLeish saw, is that it moves "at the point where the poetic revolution crosses the revolution in the social and political and economic structure of the post-war world, which so deeply concerns our generation in this country."

The phrasing of MacLeish's best-known essay on the poet's responsibilities, "The Irresponsibles" (1940), cements the relationship between his theory and his practice by calling to mind *The Fall of the City*. The announcer's description

> They wish to be free of their freedom:
> released from their liberty: —
> The long labor of liberty ended!
> They lie there.

is echoed in MacLeish's concern for the great number of men who "wish passionately and even violently to give up the long labor of liberty and surrender their wills and their bodies and even their minds to the will of a leader . . ." The division of intellectual responsibility into two castes — the scholars and the writers — meant that neither had to accept responsibility for the common culture or its defense. That past has become divorced from the present. "Where the man of letters of other centuries quarried his learning from the past to build the present, the modern scholar quarries his learning from the past to dig the quarries." The modern writer's devotion is to the thing observed "as a god sees it — without morality, without care, without judgement." Both writer and scholar, paralleling the theme of *The Fall of the City*, "freed themselves of the personal responsibility associated with personal choice . . . and by that sublimation of the mind they prepared the mind's disaster." MacLeish's essay provoked sharp and bitter responses by those who felt they had been unfairly treated. But his concern for the future of man both in his essays and in *The Fall of the City* and *Air Raid* can be seen as central reflections of the politics of the late thirties, and also of the balance MacLeish saw as necessary between the private and public worlds of the poet.

MacLeish became much more of a public figure during the latter half of Roosevelt's administration. He was appointed Librarian of Congress in 1939, assistant director of the Office of War Information in 1942, Assistant Secretary of State in 1944, and in 1946 was active in the organization of UNESCO. Still he maintained his role as writer, analyzing the strengths and weaknesses of his country as it passed through the trauma of war. One note he consistently sounded through this period was the warning that Americans continued to define peace merely as the absence of war rather than defining or developing the ideals that would lead them in the years ahead.

In *The Trojan Horse* (1952), a verse drama for radio first presented on the BBC, MacLeish again turned to eloquent mythopoeic parallels which pointed out the danger in this lack of a positive national definition. The voice of that danger held an echo of the war so recently ended:

> MAN: . . . Curious thing to be killed for:
> The right to choose and be happy!

MAN: Can you think of a better?

MAN: Peace! —
Peace! Order! Certainty!
Things in their proper places!
Respect for authority! Truth!

But while the play's theme challenged a multitude of deceptions
that have attempted to crumble cities or ideas from within, the
timing of this publication meant that many readers would see
it solely as a response to the insidiousness of McCarthyism. Precisely this response was suggested at the time in a publisher's
note, which MacLeish quotes at the beginning of his new
preface.

What Paul Brooks said then about the play was both useful
and true, but his introduction tends to forget that its author is
poet rather than politician. Just as the true focus of *Panic* is on
the street people who give to the play whatever degree of heroism
it has, so the tragic figures in *The Trojan Horse* are the dupes
willing to bow down before the values of peace and order regard-
less of the cost to human spirit. The poet's role, as MacLeish
has often said, is not to describe his time but to discover it. And
in this play the poet's intention is not only to condemn Mc-
Carthy as the danger he undoubtedly was, but to point out the
universal danger of the most profound of deceptions: corruption
from within. Had *The Trojan Horse* been written in the thirties
an editor might well have pointed to parallels with fascism or
communism. In the seventies an editor might have drawn parallels with Nixon's imperial presidency. In each case the editor
could have been right. But neither editor would have touched
on the heart of the play.

The final play in this volume reflects a poet who has moved
back from the public, or at least the political, stage to explore
the insights of his own more personal world. *This Music Crept
by Me upon the Waters* (1953) revolves around Elizabeth's

moment of true perception. Her awareness of absolute beauty parallels Ferdinand's experience in *The Tempest*, where the music that crept by him upon the waters allays both his fury and his passion with its sweet air. A more recent parallel is Eliot's *Burnt Norton* where, after the moment of intense awareness in the rose garden, the poet observes "human kind/cannot bear very much reality." And MacLeish himself in "Words in Time," one of the new poems included in *Collected Poems 1917–1952*, described this moment of awareness when "light and sound and all reply," the moment which

> The poet with a beat of words
> Flings into time for time to keep.

A similar awareness of the moment gradually becomes more evident in MacLeish's personal love poems of this period, which explore present happiness in the form of a union enveloping both present and past feeling.

From one perspective or another, all six of these plays have developed MacLeish's concern with what in *Nobodaddy* he called the theme of "self-consciousness in an indifferent universe." *Nobodaddy* treated of man's discovery of himself. *Panic, Air Raid*, and *The Fall of the City* explored concepts that have threatened man's freedom both in America and elsewhere. His insight into a similar crisis in America in the early fifties gave us *The Trojan Horse*. And in *This Music Crept by Me upon the Waters* MacLeish, with a poet's net of words, captured an individual's awareness of her relationship to reality. These plays can be read as portraits of their times, explorations of assorted themes of the thirties, forties, and fifties. Yet as we move farther away from the events that gave these works their initial impetus we begin to see MacLeish's poetic and dramatic vision more clearly. On each occasion, he has offered his understanding and insight into the human condition at those moments when universal values have been shaken. In his more recent plays, *J.B.* (1956), *Herakles* (1967), and *Scratch* (1971), as MacLeish has used biblical, classical, and American folk mythology to explore what it means to be human, this poetic and dramatic vision has continued to speak eloquently, even nobly, to us.

Edward Mullaly

Nobodaddy

Preface

To John Milton and to the Christian churches, most of them, the story of Eden in the Book of Genesis is the story of the Creation and the Fall:

> *Of man's first disobedience and the fruit*
> *Of that forbidden tree whose mortal taste*
> *Brought death into the world and all our woe . . .*

But myths change as the world changes and the events of the last centuries, the last generations, even the last few years, have altered Genesis as they have altered everything else. It is now known that humankind began, not, as in Genesis, with man, but with the stirring in the primal ooze which became man long, long after.

And because the story of Eden is no longer true it does not follow that it is no longer myth — only that its myth may have other meanings. If it is no longer the myth of the creation of man from the clay, it may be the myth of the creation of man from the animal — the myth of the beginnings of human consciousness — of that world beyond the world which exists only in ourselves but contains the universe: the whole of space; the whole of time.

This play was written in that belief fifty years ago. It is rewritten for radio now in the same conviction — in a conviction, indeed, far stronger. For "the tree of the knowledge of good and evil," which stands at the center of Eden in the story, is now, after our tragic century, no longer the fantasy it was in my younger years, but a dark, ambiguous reality against the actual sky. What fruit did Hitler eat? Or Stalin? Or we ourselves who used that murderous miracle at Hiroshima? The monstrous terrorists who save the world by slaughter? The criminal children in our rotting cities?

As we once read the Book of Genesis back at the beginning of the century, Adam and Eve were forbidden to eat the fruit of the tree of the knowledge of good and evil because they would become gods if they did. The serpent puts it bluntly. God knows, he says, that "on the day you eat your eyes shall be opened and ye shall be as gods knowing good and evil." And Blake (who referred to the god of Eden as Nobodaddy) drew the same conclusion in his time:

> *Why art thou silent and invisible*
> *Father of jealousy?*
> *Why dost thou hide thyself in clouds . . .*
>
> *Why darkness and obscurity*
> *In all thy words and laws*
> *That none dare eat the fruit but from*
> *The wily serpent's jaws?*

But is Blake right *now*? Is divine jealousy the motive as *we* read the story? Was it to keep Adam and Eve from becoming gods that they were forbidden the fruit that would open their eyes? Or was it to keep them safe in that garden, that green, golden innocence mankind has always half remembered — the eternal *now* of nature which has no time for human consciousness?

We in our generation know the longing for that garden — the yearning to return. We think continually of the lovely peaceful past: the white New England churches, the red barns. We can well understand that a god who loved us might have wished to save us from the knowledge that has brought us where we are. But, though we long to go back, we read the story these days to the end.

For the story, of course, goes on — has always gone on — into the desert. It does not end with the Fall — the loss of Eden — the slowly turning sword before the gate. Cain must still be born in the harsh land and after Cain his brother Abel and Abel's offering must be accepted by God and Cain's rejected and Cain must murder Abel and bear the curse of God: "a fugitive and a vagabond shalt thou be in the earth."

A fugitive and a wanderer, yes. One who knows himself and sees his death before him and the desert all around. Cain, the son of those whose eyes were opened. The murderer of the brother whose offering was accepted. He who will not go back again to Eden. Who would not, even if he could. Who will go on. Who has the journey of mankind before him and the myth of man to bear.

A. MacL.

5

A prelude of midsummer music, flooded with sun and air and the sound of leaves. It breaks off. A bird's song. Another. The first again. Three together. Four. Five. Then, suddenly and all at once, silence, and through the silence, like a runnel of quick water in the grass, a sliding sound.

THE SOUND:
So . . .

MAN'S VOICE: (*sleepy*)
Ah, no! No! Go away.

THE SOUND:
Sleeping, Adam?

ADAM:
When you let me.

THE SOUND:
Why are you always sleeping, Adam?

ADAM:
Because you're always waking me from sleep.
I know you . . . Serpent!

6

SERPENT:
                           You don't know me.
You've never even seen me, Adam.
You lie there with your sleepy arm
over your sleepy eyelids . . .

(*silence*)

                                Why not
look at it, Adam?

ADAM:
                    Look at what?

SERPENT:
                           The tree.

(*Wind. A deep humming of wind in tree leaves: a live, deep, vivid, vibrant humming.*)

SERPENT: (*through the humming of the leaves*)
The tree of the knowledge of good and evil, Adam.

(*The humming dies away.*)

The forbidden tree!

(*a snicker of laughter*)

                           The tree forbidden to
you, Adam.

ADAM:
                    Leave me alone.

SERPENT:
Why is the tree of the knowledge of good and evil
forbidden to you, Adam?

(*pause*)

7

Because of the good?

(*pause*)

Of course not.

(*pause*)

Because of the evil?

(*pause*)

Is there evil?

(*snicker of laughter*)

Because of what then? — of the knowledge?
The knowledge of good? The knowledge of evil?
But whose knowledge, Adam?

(*pause*)

Yours?

(*a long pause*)

Is it you yourself you must not know?

(*A violent humming in the leaves. An almost uttering of almost words. It dies away.*)

So you won't look at the tree, Adam?

ADAM:

I've looked at it.

SERPENT:
Or touch it either?

ADAM:

There are other trees.

8

SERPENT:
And as for the apples . . . ?

You're not hungry.

(*pause*)

Still . . . you dare not eat them, Adam.

ADAM:
I do not wish to die.

SERPENT:

Who talked of dying?

ADAM:
God. He made me. When He wills . . .
When He wills He can unmake me.

SERPENT:
Cannot, Adam. Cannot undo what He has
done — untie one knot of His creation —
think again one thought. Have you not seen
how in the morning He obeys His sun
to come into His orchard, and how slow
He follows His slow seasons round the wall?
Have you not seen how sometimes He has failed
and would go back but cannot? There are things
crawling beneath the stones and under earth,
white stinging worms and venomous soft slugs,
that were to be as lovely as the quick
green lizards. Have you not seen Him look,
turning a stone up in His gardening,
as though He would destroy the world and then
let down the stone as gently as He drops
dust on his seedlings? Have you watched Him
working all day to keep the briars down
and then, at dusk, the flowering of the briars?
Have you not seen it, Adam?

9

ADAM:
                              I have seen
His Behemoth, His monster, fall and die
among the reeds where Hiddekel flows out.

SERPENT:
    Ah, did you see it? Wonderful! What apple
    had God forbidden him to eat? You fool!
    Behemoth was His greatest and God loves
    His greatest most. Ten thousand years he grew
    lifting his stupid head above the palms,
    and then, because it rained one summer, died,
    and when God found him He would not believe
    the bones were Behemoth.

ADAM:
                              But still he died.

SERPENT:
    But still he died. Yes, and the sun itself
    will die some day — in spite of God.

ADAM:
                              Listen!

(*slow, heavy, distant steps*)

SERPENT:
    He walks among His olive trees to pluck
    the spotted and sick fruit. Even among
    His olive tree He fails sometimes.

ADAM:
                              Be quiet.
    If He should call to me —

SERPENT:
                              He cannot hear us.

And if He did He would not understand
two words together.

(*trill of laughter*)

                His sense is always filled
and ringing with the rumour of small leaves
and drip of water sifting through the ground,
and stir of earth where the young seedling heaves
its tip to sunlight, and the swarming sound
the wind makes in the meadow grass that weaves
sound over movement and runs down the green
flashing and singing and yet never seen.
He does not listen to me, does not hear me . . .
any more than grass hears moonlight.

ADAM:

                            He can
speak. And when I hear that heavy thunder
circling the sullen sky I am afraid.

SERPENT:
Afraid! But you are *Adam.*

ADAM:

                What is Adam?

SERPENT:
If you had eaten of the tree, you'd know . . .
You'd see.

ADAM:

        See what?

SERPENT:

            See Adam.

ADAM:

                I have seen him.

SERPENT:
   And Eve . . . whom you have never seen.

ADAM:
   I see her everywhere she goes, and she goes
everywhere — wherever I go — follows me.

SERPENT:
   You've never even looked at her, poor Adam.
Never known her — what she is.
You are forbidden knowledge, Adam.
Have you forgotten what He told you?
You are forbidden knowledge of yourself . . .
and her.

   (*a rustling of leaves*)

ADAM:
       Listen.

SERPENT:
         It's only Eve . . .
                who follows.

ADAM:
   Because I do not wish to die, you laugh at me.

SERPENT:
   Because you need not die.

ADAM:
             The day you
eat of it, He said . . .

EVE:
       Adam!
What are you saying, Adam? What are you saying?
Why do you lie there, talking to yourself?

ADAM:

Not to myself — the serpent.

EVE:

What did he
say? — the serpent?

ADAM:

Terrible dark words.

EVE:

What words? How terrible? What did he say of
me? What have you done to make him angry?
I bring him milk when I remember and he loves me.
What did he say to you?

ADAM:

He says I'm Adam.

EVE:

Of course you're Adam. You're warm, brown Adam
and your beard's like lamb's wool and you lie as still
beside me as the woodmice when you're good
and when you're bad you pinch me . . .

ADAM:

Not
that kind of Adam.

EVE:

What kind?

ADAM:

Oh,
Adam when he shall know he's Adam.

EVE:

But you
know.

13

ADAM:
The serpent does not say so.
The serpent says, when I have eaten . . .

EVE:
And God says, that day we will surely die.

ADAM:
The serpent says we won't die . . .

EVE:
God . . .

ADAM:
God thinks the way the days go — on and on —
yesterday, today, tomorrow.
He cannot kill us. He cannot go back.
What He has done is done. What follows follows.
Everything that will be has been willed before.
He made us. He cannot unmake us.

EVE:
You believe that?

ADAM:
I don't know.
I believe the tree is what God called it.
I believe the fruit has been forbidden us —
that the knowledge of good and evil has been forbidden us.
I believe that if we ate we'd know.
But whether God would kill us if we ate,
or we, if we should know, would kill . . .

EVE:
Know what?

ADAM:
Ourselves — our choices — everything.

14

(The sliding sound. It moves through the grass — silence.)

EVE:

The serpent heard us and he's gone.

ADAM:

Or else a bird . . .

EVE:

                    Are you afraid the
birds might tell Him?

ADAM:

              I don't know.

EVE:

If we should taste — just taste — one apple.
See, there are two together on that branch.
He'd never know there had been two.
Pull the branch down, Adam.

(rustle of leaves; the humming sound)

ADAM:

                  Listen!
As though the tree were warning us . . .

EVE:

                        Or welcoming.

There!

ADAM:

        Wait! Don't pluck it.

EVE:

                Ah!

(the humming louder, almost shrill now)

                    It tastes like . . .
What does it taste like, Adam?

ADAM:

I don't
know. Like . . .

EVE:

Light!

ADAM:

How can it taste like
light?

EVE:

It does though. And we do not die.
Nothing changes . . .

nothing changes . . .

Adam!
Why do you look so, Adam? You make me
shiver when you look at me like that.
No — you hurt me, Adam. Adam!

(*the humming louder, nearer*)

You look at me as though I were not you —
not part of you, not taken from your side —
What can I be if I am not your bone,
your flesh, as God has made me? What can I
be?

ADAM:

You can be Eve.

(*the humming louder; a small cry — hers*)

You are Eve!
·Eve!

(*The humming changes to not quite music, not quite singing:
human — a deeper, a more human sound.*)

16

EVE:

Sleep, Adam.

ADAM:

I cannot sleep. I hear the
tree. It tries to speak to me. I cannot
understand it, Eve, I cannot . . .

EVE:

Cover your ears with my hair, Adam.
Cover your ears with my hair. Sleep!
What does it matter if you understand or
not? We've eaten . . . Sleep!

(*The sound of the tree fades into silence, a long silence. Nothing. Absolute silence — and then, secretly, a sound — a small, slow sound of something, someone moving through the fern, then stopping, standing, not quite still. Then, suddenly a crash of sound. Adam is on his feet. We hear his breathing.*)

ADAM:

He was *here!* I saw Him.

EVE: (*drowsy*)

In your sleep . . .
You were asleep, poor Adam, and you dreamed it.
Lie down. Put your arms around me. There,
that's better.

(*a sigh — Adam's; silence*)

ADAM:

But He *was.* He stood there looking
down the way the stars do and not seeing.
Eve, He cannot see us any longer.
He looked at me. He did not *see!*

17

EVE:
                                    Poor
Adam! But *we* see. We see the constellations.
Look, there's stupid camel overhead
balancing his tiny skull
atop his neck-bone like a melon . . .

(*pause*)

And Ibis perched upon her one pink stalk
letting the light fall all around . . .

(*Her voice breaks.*)

                              Why won't you
answer, Adam? Hold me. I'm afraid.

ADAM:
I'm listening. There's something moving — someone . . .

EVE:
You hear the bittern in the marsh.

ADAM:
I hear God's footstep in the forest.

EVE:
But we haven't died. We took the apple
and we slept and now we've wakened.

ADAM:
I think it's not from sleep we've wakened.
I think it's Eden we have wakened from
and nothing else that lives there, even
God Himself, has wakened with us . . .

(*pause*)

I think we are awake alone and cannot
sleep again in Eden.

EVE:
                    Where are you
going, Adam? Oh, come back.

ADAM:
                          God!
Speak to me, God! Where are You . . .

(*echo*)

                          Are You . . .

ADAM: (*his voice farther and farther*)
Now that I see myself can You not see me?
Will You not speak, now I have spoken?

EVE:
Wait, Adam!

(*her running step*)

             Wait for me!
                 Oh Adam!

ADAM:
We cannot stay here, Eve.
                   We cannot stay.
Everything in Eden turns its
being from us — even God
Whose eyes no longer meet our eyes. When we were
His and lived within His silver will as
spiders do within the webs He makes them,
He would speak to us. Now He is silent.
He passes us by night and cannot see.

EVE:
Where can we go? Beyond the garden
only desert everywhere . . .

ADAM:
> Then desert.

(The music of the prelude but no longer a music of high summer and of singing leaves: of wind now and blowing sand and blazing sky. Years of wind and sand and desert. The music ends. A bleating of goats. The pounding of a mattock in baked earth. Voices: Eve's first, older. Then Cain's, a grown man.)

EVE:
There once was water, Cain — an ooze of water —
a slow, brown ooze of water. I remember
Adam pressing down his heel
just where your mattock is and waiting
and when the ooze had filled his footprint, I would drink.
Then *he* would . . . after . . .

(thud of the mattock; grunting blows)

> You were not born then.

(thud of the mattock; the wind)

When your father died you found the
wadi and the water underground
and dug your well and then your brother Abel
brought his goats home and you fenced your garden.

CAIN: *(thud of the mattock)*
And now it has not rained for seven years
and there are thorn trees in the well instead of water.

(thud of the mattock; angry blow)

I'll dig another if I have to . . .

(thud of the mattock)

> and another.

EVE:
Abel says he saw a cloud this morning.

CAIN:
Over Eden. There are always clouds there.
The garden god takes care of that —
the god of green and growing; god
to whom a living, thinking man is
only one more seed, another root,
ignorant root, obedient blind seed.
"Thou shalt not know," he said. Adam was
right to disobey him. If it never
rains here in the world again I'll break the
rocks for water and dig down and down
until I know what earth is — what I *am.*

EVE:
Abel does not think as you do.

CAIN:
                              Ah! —
Abel!

EVE:
          He used to ask me every night
If we could go to Eden in the morning —
back to Eden. He was little then.

CAIN:
And talked to stones.

EVE:
                    Yes, and said they answered him.

CAIN: (*The sound of the mattock stops.*)
Eve! Did they answer *you?*

(*pause*)

21

No, tell me —
Did they?
When you lived in Eden in the will of God?

EVE:
I cannot tell you, Cain. I think of it.
I think but I cannot remember.
Is Abel what we were? I do not know.

CAIN:
And I — I cannot think of it. I'm Cain —
never anything but Cain, but humankind,
born of disobedience in the desert,
the earth my enemy to break and teach —
the sky against me and my self to find.

EVE:
And God? You think that God's against you?

CAIN:
Not *against* me. Elsewhere. His slow thought
is like the sap in orchards. When He thinks in
trees they blossom or their leaves grow green,
and when He thinks in Abel, Abel hunts
or sleeps or wanders off or doesn't.
God cannot think in me. He does not know me.
But I — I, Cain — shall come to know.

EVE:
You are my son and I am Eve — earth's daughter.
Earthy things are in me that, at rains,
touch me to the heart with longing. They touch you.
We will destroy ourselves if we tear out
our roots from earth.

CAIN:
And if we live like roots
we will destroy ourselves. We are not trees but

men and it was you who made us — you, not
God — you and my father, Adam, who is dead.

EVE:
Cain! Hush, Cain!

CAIN:
What is it?

EVE:
Abel.
He has the ram upon his shoulder.

CAIN:
Yes, and the look his eyes have in the night —
that look of . . . listening . . . a silence in his eyes.

EVE:
Abel, they say it rains in Eden . . .
Abel.

ABEL:
Yes, in the night it rained there, I have been
as far as where you see the sword that turns
though no hand turns it.

CAIN: (*startled*)
When!

ABEL:
I am just come.

EVE:
What did you see there, Abel?

ABEL:
Green.

CAIN:
Yes, green,
green leaves in Eden. But was — no one there?

ABEL:

There was a wind there. Wind! There was a wind —
it came to meet me. I was in the wind.
It came to call to me: I came, I came . . .
No, there was no one there. I called to Him.
I called His name. But He was not in Eden.
So then I knew where He had gone, and now —
now I shall speak to Him.

CAIN:

                           You must speak loud:
the sky is farther off than Eden.

ABEL:

                                    No,
He will come here to me.

CAIN:

                           And you will tell Him
it does not rain enough?

EVE:

                    Why will He come?

ABEL:

Because the ram's blood dripping on the earth
shall call Him.

CAIN:

                    You will not kill the ram!

ABEL:

Why not? It's my ram. I have reared it.

CAIN:

                                    Yes,
it is yours.

24

ABEL:
     Why shall I not?

CAIN:
                         The ram has done
nothing to harm you. It is not the ram
that brings the drouth here, Abel.

ABEL:
                              But his blood,
because he is my best, will end it. Look!
there is no mark upon him and his horns
are beautiful.

CAIN:
          God will rejoice to smell
the blood of a dead ram. He will be glad.
I think He will, my brother, for He makes
hands that can spill it.

ABEL:
                    What will *you* give?
What will you offer God?

CAIN:
                    I have my beans
killed in the drouth He sends us. Will they please Him?
Or shall I offer Him the withered corn
that rattles in the wind its dry dead bones?
He has destroyed it all.

ABEL:
                    You do not speak
the thing your eyes say, Cain. You do not love Him.
You hate Him in your eyes. But when He comes . . .

EVE:
What will you say to Him, Abel, when He comes?
What will you ask Him.

25

ABEL:

To go back.

CAIN:

Back? Into Eden? To the womb we came from?

ABEL:

Back into the will of God.

CAIN:

You cannot.
Neither to the one nor to the other.
Adam knew that.

ABEL:

Adam died.

CAIN:

And knew before he died what Adam was.

ABEL:

Knew what *God* is — God Whose wrath
dries the earth to ashes, scorches
leaves . . . the trees are winnowed.

CAIN:

And you'd kill your ram
to quiet the dry rage of God? You dare not.
Only God can kill the things that trust Him.

I say you dare not, Abel . . .

(*sound of a blow*)

No! No! Ah, Abel, look. His blood spurts out.
See, it is on my hands, it burns.

ABEL:

Kneel down!

(*in a low monotone*)

26

Drink, earth. You were thirsty, earth. I give you drink.
I am the son of Adam, hear me, earth.
I am the ram's blood; drink, O drink me, earth.
Through all your veins, throughout your secret veins
let me be poured, O let me cry in you.
Let me flood inward where the hidden one
waits at the root of darkness; where the word
is uttered darkly let my voice be heard,
until He hears, until He speaks to me.

CAIN:

Something I know — something I half remember
that reaches hands to me to drag me down
groveling. Blood — of a ram. I do not fear it.
I say I do not fear it. I will stand
although the trees fall down to Him. Cry out,
cry louder, Abel, He is far away;
cry till you split your throat. He cannot hear you.

(*wind rises*)

ABEL:

I am your lover, Earth. Why are you still?
I am your lover, do you know me not?
Have you forgotten how, on Gihon's hill,
at midday on the treeless hill, the hot
bare hill of Gihon, the expectant thrill
of fingers moving — did you answer then?
And will not now? And will not speak again?

CAIN:

As though my body, tied still to the womb
that feeds it — that has food for me no more —
cried out! O Abel, crying to the earth,
You are the bond that binds me, the dumb fear

that beats me down. I will go free of you,
break through this Abel in me and go free.

(*distant thunder*)

ABEL:

Wind in the faint sky.
                    Do you answer me?
Wind and the birds cry.
                    Do you speak to me?
Wind on the desert with lagging feet.
                            Oh come!
Wind upon the wilderness with hurrying beat.
                                Oh come!
Shiver of wind in the gray dead grasses.
                            Near!
Rustle of leaves where the fresh wind passes.
                            Here!
Swirl of windy shimmering slashing through the trees
and rain, rain, rain. He has heard! He sees!

EVE:

Abel! He has answered, Abel.

CAIN:

He has not answered *me*. He took
everything . . . and has not answered.

ABEL:

He always answers. And the Lord said unto Cain:
Why art thou wroth and why is thy countenance fallen?
If thou doest well shalt thou not be accepted?
And if thou doest not well . . .

CAIN:

Did Abel do well? He killed the ram that trusted him:
his sacrifice has been accepted.

But I — I did not well. I gave you
nothing when you'd taken all.

(*pause*)

I do not know your well and your not well.
All I know is will — your will. Oh, let me
go! Sever this thick vein that binds my
body to the body of my brother.

EVE:

Cain! Put the knife down, Cain! Put down the
knife!

(*a shriek; a raging gust of wind; the rain*)

You have killed him!

(*dead silence*)

Oh, my sons!

(*The gust passes; the rain comes.*)

Abel, there was a name you called me
once, before you learned to hate my name.
Speak to me, Abel . . .

(*the rain*)

No. Not now. Not ever.

(*the rain*)

Cain! Cain! Cain! What have you
done?

CAIN:

Killed.

EVE:

Worse than killed! Killed your

29

brother!

(*silence; the rain*)

You know now what you are.

CAIN:
I know.

EVE:
Cain who has murdered Abel.

CAIN:
Beyond the garden of the will of God,
past the dry well in the desert,
farther than the slaughtered ram —
farther even than the murdered brother . . .

(*The music begins . . . waits . . . falters . . . breaks off.*)

Cain! who weeps . . .
who has become a man . . .

(*the music*)

THE END

30

Panic

Preface

The one memorable circumstance associated with the New York production of *Panic* in 1935 was the fact that it played for three nights, not for two. It was a handsome Phoenix Theater production with Orson Welles and Martha Graham and her famous chorus. Jimmy Light of the Provincetown directed. John Houseman produced. But the play was about the Great Depression and the Great Depression was in its sixth unendurable year and no one wanted to look at it, on a stage or anywhere else. That was obvious on opening night and more than obvious on the night that followed, and we would have stopped then and there if the editors of *The New Masses* and some of their Marxist friends had not made us an offer. They would fill the house for a third night if the author would submit himself to questioning after the final curtain.

The author, of course, agreed: we had bills to pay. And when the final curtain fell on a decent silence relieved by a little perfunctory applause, it promptly rose again to reveal a row of interrogators seated on the stage and the author in a chair apart wondering what the charges against him would turn out to be. He soon found out.

The interrogators, like most beginning Marxists of the twenties and thirties, believed — believed devoutly — in Rosa Luxemburg's doctrine of historical determinism whereas the author clearly didn't. Which is to say that the interrogators believed that history was made by immutable laws divulged by suitable oracles while the author continued to put his trust in the Jeffersonian doctrine that history is made by men. And this difference, needless to say, affected their respective views of the Great Depression. To the interrogators, the Great Depression proved the truth of historical determinism: the Pytho of London had foretold the inevitable collapse of capitalism and here it was collapsing, taking self-government and the private activities of human beings with it. The author, on the other hand, saw the Great Depression as the consequence, not of Marx's oracular revelations, but of human stupidity and cowardice and greed: he even went so far as to quote Mr. Roosevelt's observation that we had nothing to fear but fear itself, meaning that men, as they had caused the Depression, could put an end to it themselves if they could find the courage.

The staged discussion, in other words, was not enlightening because minds never met. What the interrogators wanted to discuss was the imminent fall of a republic which was about to rise to its greatest triumph: the destruction of Hitler. I, on the contrary, wanted to talk about my unheroic hero, the aging tycoon McGafferty, who had lost his nerve as he had lost his love because he no longer believed in himself.

I don't remember how the evening ended — who called it off or who left first — but I know I walked back home to the Village thinking of Rosa Luxemburg and most particularly of her ominous phrase, "objective historical necessity." The Greeks too had known Necessity. They had made her the mother of the Fates and therefore the dowager of destiny. If the great, new Revolution of the Proletariat had turned its back on the American Revolution of Mankind to revert to the world of oracles and omens, we had indeed nothing to fear but fear itself. Which was the most encouraging thought I had had that evening. But yet, and even so, there was my McGafferty. Could we trust him not to throw himself from his skyscraper window again?

A. MacL.

PRELUDE

Clattering rush of a subway express train. Click of the wheels on the points. The counterpoint beat of a steel-shod cane on the iron floor. A man's voice speaking an unintelligible word over and over as it draws nearer. We hear the words "blind" . . . "blind man" . . .

BLIND MAN:
The blind man, please . . .
                              Excuse the blind man . . .

(*the voice nearer*)

BLIND MAN:
Excuse me, madame. I beg your pardon.
I see with my hands.

WOMAN:
                              Not on *my* face!

BLIND MAN:
No. Not yours.

MAN: (*deep voice; old*)
                              Nor mine, for God's sake.

(*The beat of the cane stops.*)

36

BLIND MAN:
Ah! It's you. Mister McGafferty . . .
Owner of everything on earth.
The famous financier. McGafferty!
I was looking for you, Mister McGafferty.

MCGAFFERTY:
Well, you've found me. What do you want?

BLIND MAN:
Not what you want, Mister McGafferty.
Nevertheless we ride together.
Indeed we're almost there.

MCGAFFERTY:
                    We?

BLIND MAN:
Almost. At the end of everything.
End for you. Where you get off.

(no reply; rush of the train; clack of the wheels.)

Listen! You hear the wheels, McGafferty?
They're talking to you. "Factories closing."
"Farms foreclosed." "Credits frozen."
"Billions in banks and the bank doors closed."

(The train slows down.)

MCGAFFERTY:
Let me pass, sir.

BLIND MAN:
                    You don't hear them.
"Great Depression" you think they say.
It's something more than that, McGafferty.
You know your Marx. You've read the prophecy:
you and your kind dead and done for;

37

the Great Republic on its failed foundation
fallen, ruined, rotted, lost.
Liberty, that rank delusion!

(*The train has stopped. The doors hiss open. A rush of heels and voices.*)

MCGAFFERTY:
  Let me pass, sir!

BLIND MAN:
                    I don't stop you.
  How can I stop *you*, McGafferty?
  I a blind man?
                    But fate can.
  Destiny has spoken and you stand there.
  History's necessity commands you.
  Marx has prophesied and you believe him.
  You spit upon his name but you believe him.
  You mean to die, McGafferty. You will.
  You and your Republic — your free land.
  You don't trust your freedom now. You stand there.

Hiss of the doors closing. The clatter of the wheels begins. The rush of the train — a great and rising roar that swallows itself — diminishes into the sound of the typewriters in McGafferty's office at the beginning of the play.

*

An inner office. Muted sound of office equipment — typewriters, telephone buzzers, copying machines — heard through a closed door. The sudden frantic chatter of a news-ticker. It breaks off as abruptly as it began.

SECRETARIAL VOICE: (*on a public address system*)
  Mr. Immelman. Mr. Immelman.
  Mr. McGafferty is asking for Mr. Immelman.

(The sound of the machines increases as a door is opened. It is muted again as the door closes.)

IMMELMAN: *(a dry, impersonal, functionary voice)*
You asked for me, Mr. McGafferty.

MCGAFFERTY:
That yammering ticker. What's happened now?

IMMELMAN:
Seaman's National. Detroit.

MCGAFFERTY:
Closed?

IMMELMAN:
     Closed.

MCGAFFERTY:
         Makes nineteen banks today.

IMMELMAN:
Not only banks. Plants. Factories.
Payrolls up to fifty thousand.
Fifty thousand men, not dollars.

MCGAFFERTY:
All today.

IMMELMAN:
     All today.
Each day like the last.

MCGAFFERTY:
         Or worse.

IMMELMAN:
Or worse.

MCGAFFERTY:
>   Three years of it.

IMMELMAN:
>   And more:
> four since nineteen twenty-nine.

MCGAFFERTY:
> And why? Nobody can tell you why.
> The most productive, vigorous economy
> anywhere on earth and all at once
> crumbling like a castle made of sand.
> There never was technology like ours,
> labor like our labor, farm land
> richer than our farms in Illinois,
> in Iowa, Wisconsin. Now we're hungry.
> Hungry! And the dollar dwindling
> payday after payday. And for God's sake
> why? Economists can't tell you.
> All they know is that their graphs turn down.
> Depressed. So that's the answer — a depression.
> But why are all their graphs depressed?
> They just don't know. They've heard that brokers
> fall from open windows ten floors up —
> that soup lines in the snow grow longer.
> They've seen their college classmates selling pencils.
> They read the papers probably. They still don't
> know. And now the banks are closing . . .

(silence)

IMMELMAN:
> Will that be all, sir?

MCGAFFERTY:
>   Yes.

(*a laugh*)

Forgive me.

Call Detroit and ask if there is anything . . .
There won't be . . .

anything this bank can do.

IMMELMAN: (*at the telephone*)
Get me Seaman's National in Detroit . . .
Henderson if you can reach him . . . Urgent . . .
No. No. I'll hold on . . .

(A *door opens — evidently not the door to the outer office.
The machines are still muted.*)

A WOMAN'S VOICE: (*young, warm, amused*)
Oh, I'm sorry. I came up the stairs.
Shall I go down again?

MCGAFFERTY:

Come in.

IMMELMAN: (*on the phone*)
Is that you, Henderson?

MCGAFFERTY:

I said, Come in.

IMMELMAN:
Have him call me. Immelman. New York.

MCGAFFERTY:
You've met Mr. Immelman, Ione?

IONE:
I think we've . . . bowed. How are you?

IMMELMAN: (*stiffly*)

Yes. We've . . .

bowed. Well . . . I'll be going . . .

41

IONE:
Don't be going. I'll go.

MCGAFFERTY:
No. Sit down.

IMMELMAN:
Henderson will call tomorrow. So . . .
Good night.

IONE: (*too sweetly*)
Must you? Then good night.

(*The door to the outer office opens: sound of the machines. The door closes.*)

IONE:
Good night!

(*silence*)

I thought you'd never come so I came.

(*silence*)

The years I've waited for six — for six-thirty . . .

(*silence*)

God, you're responsive!

MCGAFFERTY:
Dull. I know. I'm sorry.
Almost the worst day I remember.
I'm getting old, Ione — older.

IONE:
Yes,
like oak, and all the better for it.
Tell me what happened. Immelman?

MCGAFFERTY:
No. Me. I'm done for. No one tell you?

IONE:

No one tells me anything. Who says so?

MCGAFFERTY:

A blind man says so. On the subway.
Dead and done for. And not only me —
everything, the whole shebang:
the country, the economy, the works.
History's through with us: destiny's caught up:
the revolution of mankind is finished:
The Great Republic is undone . . .

IONE:

How do you suppose he knows?

MCGAFFERTY:

                                    He knows.
Everything knows. Even the stock market.
Even the mortgaged farms — the banks.
They close like bars at midnight — all together.

IONE:

It's beautiful, darling. Don't you think it's beautiful?
Mr. McGafferty dead and done for!
Richest man in the world. Most powerful.

MCGAFFERTY:

Beautiful? No. I wouldn't say so.
Ever feel a blind man's fingers,
smooth as cicatrices, brush your face?

IONE:

Blind, and he could find you in that crowd?

MCGAFFERTY:

He found me anyway — came pressing through
holding his blind man's cane and touched me —
bowed to me. Quite a gentleman he was —

43

cool, well-spoken, courteous even.
I had no choice but listen to him.
I mean I had no *choice*. Like people
listening in those old Greek plays:
Tiresias speaks — they *have* to listen.

IONE:
Listen and believe?

MCGAFFERTY:
                              Ah, that's the question.
In the plays they had to . . .
                                        at the end.

IONE:
Forgive me. I've been stupid.

MCGAFFERTY:
                              No, not stupid.
You've always laughed. Why not? I think you'd take it
laughing if I told you that the worst
he prophesied was happening — may happen.

IONE:
How *should* I take it with your name in bronze
on all this marble? Oh, I'll cry
but not for fortunetellers.

MCGAFFERTY:
                              Nor for love?
Old men in love are always to be laughed at —
particularly when they lose their crowns,
their kingdoms, everything they have.

IONE:
                                        You think I
laugh at love — *your* love?
                              Is it not *mine*?

44

(*pause*)

Am I the cheap and purchasable whore
who gives her willingness but not her will?
I never gave my love yet but my pride
in being loved went with it and before.
I only give my mouth where it can praise.

MCGAFFERTY:

Yes. And when the praise is over?

IONE:

Oh, I'm more calculating than you think:
I choose the praise that lasts. When mine for you
is gone there'll be no breath or mouth to
give to anyone for anything . . .

(*the stammer and whir of the news-ticker*)

MCGAFFERTY:

Look at me, Ione. You
who need the weight of fame to feel
an old man's body on your body —
what would you feel now if the fame were gone?
Loathing of the man who'd loved you?

(*the ticker louder; the beat more violent*)

IONE:

It is not like you to have said those words —
no, nor not like me to listen to them —
not like either of us to have heard or said.

(*knock*)

MCGAFFERTY:

Come in!

(*louder*)

      Come in!

(A door opens: clatter and whir of the ticker.)

IMMELMAN:

I thought you ought to see this . . .

(The door closes, muffling the frantic beat.)

MCGAFFERTY:
What have you got there? Tape?

IMMELMAN:

The last ten minutes.

MCGAFFERTY:
Read it — the essentials. *Read it!*

IMMELMAN: *(rustle of the tape as he thumbs through)*
The essentials . . .

riots in Delaware . . .

foreclosures . . .

foreclosures . . .

bankruptcies . . .

furnaces

dead now that were burning forty years . . .
moratorium . . .

MCGAFFERTY:

What?

IMMELMAN:

Moratorium —

Michigan . . .

IONE:

What does it mean?

MCGAFFERTY:

It means a

moratorium in Michigan.

46

IMMELMAN:

         . . . Tomorrow . . .
New York City . . . Savings Trust . . .
crowds of thousands gathering . . . all night vigil . . .

MCGAFFERTY:

That's enough. Call the committee.
I want all of them — the lot —
here — as soon as they can get here.

(*Immelman's running feet. The door opens: stays open.
Sound of the pounding ticker; telephone buzzers; bells; voices
reading the tape: typists, clerks, officers — men and women.*)

MAN:

Savings Trust . . . what about Savings Trust?

MAN:

Cash exhausted — cash credits exhausted —
last cash credits exhausted . . .

WOMAN:

Bankers summoned to conference . . .
Mister McGafferty summons . . .

MAN:

Government calls on McGafferty . . .

WOMAN:

Thousands gathered in throngs . . .

MAN:

Government thanks us — the government! —
keeping calm in the crisis!

WOMAN:

Our father who art Thou in Heaven
forgive us our daily bread . . .

47

MAN:
  Keeping calm in the crisis! . . .

WOMAN:
  Mister McGafferty summons . . .

WOMAN:
  What does it say? Foreclosures?
  Closing like doors in a wind
  in a dead house — abandoned . . .

WOMAN:
  Blight but not in the grain . . .

MAN:
  Drouth but not in the springs . . .

MAN:
  Rot but not from the rain . . .

MAN:
  Bankers summoned to conference.

WOMAN:
  What can bankers do?
  It's the closing of doors in the wind
  in a dead house and the stove
  cold, the kitchen abandoned.
  What can they say to the wind?
  They can't see it? Can anyone?

(*The sound of footsteps drowns the voices: heels on the hard-
wood floor, the door opening and closing, chairs pulled out,
pushed in, and at last silence — the door closed, the ticker
muffled.*)

MCGAFFERTY:
  Thank you for coming, gentlemen. So promptly.

48

BANKER:
What's all this about, McGafferty?

BANKER:
Couldn't it wait till morning? Business hours?

MCGAFFERTY:
I think you know. There's a moratorium. In Michigan.

BANKER:
Yes. In *Michigan.*

MCGAFFERTY:
And in New York
crowds are camped in the street at Savings Trust.

BANKER:
Nothing to fear but fear itself.
That's what the new man says — in Washington.

MCGAFFERTY:
You mean the President? Of the Republic?

BANKER:
Whatever you want to call him. I don't like him.

MCGAFFERTY:
Neither do I but you'll call him President.
That's what he is and we need one — badly.

BANKER:
All we have to fear is fear itself!
What does he think that mob is up at Savings?

MCGAFFERTY:
People probably. Depositors. Who want their money.

BANKER:
And what are we supposed to do?

49

BANKER:
What about you, McGafferty? What will *you* do?

MCGAFFERTY:
What do you think? Pull out? Give up?
This bank will open tomorrow at
nine and thereafter at nine and thereafter at
nine o'clock for a long spell — maybe longer.

(*crash of his fist on the table*)

What can any of us do but face it?
Prop the weak up till the worst blows over.
They'll take us with them if we don't.
Look 'round you, gentlemen! Look 'round you!
What's a hundred million at this table?
A hundred million does it — stops the run —
ends the panic. It's been done before.
Our fathers did it. And their fathers.

BANKER:
That was in our fathers' time.

BANKER:
They fought by daylight with live men —
James J. Hill and the fight for the Burlington.

BANKER:
In the old days there were plagues, floods,
famine, pestilence. We overcame them.
Now there's everything a people needs
and factories closed — towns deserted . . .

BANKER:
Jobs disappear. Money cheapens.
The hoarded fortune dwindles in the sock:
no one touches it — it dwindles:
stocks go down for nothing, for no reason.
How can you face it when there's nothing — no one?

MCGAFFERTY:

Don't tell me there's nothing there.
That's why we're sitting at this table:
we're here because there's nothing. Panic!
Fear without a name!

(*A knock; the door opens; the ticker clatters.*)

What is it, Immelman?

IMMELMAN:
Detroit. The Guardian.

BANKER:

What about the Guardian?

IMMELMAN:
Thousands crowding the doors in the dark.

BANKER:
The Guardian!

BANKER:

Even the Guardian gone, McGafferty.

BANKER:
Ever been in Michigan, McGafferty?
Ever watched the forests burning?
Seen how the pines go up in a big one,
exploding like shells — ten together or twenty or
one on a hill in a white flash — the blast of it
bumping the smoke open?

(*The door closes; the ticker is muffled.*)

You're too late, McGafferty.

BANKER:
It's every man for himself now, McGafferty.

MCGAFFERTY:
  God, you sound like girls who've seen a ghost!
  There's only will and weather in this world:
  once the will is lost the weather takes you.

BANKER:
  It's easy enough for you, McGafferty, riding the
  world with your great bank and your great fortune,
  governments begging their bread from you — easy enough!

BANKER:
  You can count us out — First National.

BANKER:
  Count the Fidelity out.

BANKER:
                    Fechtheim. Out.

MCGAFFERTY:
  All right! All right, gentlemen.
  Make it fifty million. We'll take ten . . .
  Five apiece for each of you.

BANKER:
  Count the lot of us out.

MCGAFFERTY:
                    Five million!
  You can't walk out on that.

BANKER:
                    Can't we?

BANKER:
  Watch us!

  (*Chairs are pushed back.*)

BANKER:

Watch us, McGafferty!

(*Door is opened; the ticker is louder.*)

BANKER:

Just watch!

BANKER:

It's every man for himself in a sea, McGafferty.

(*Clicking heels; the door is slammed shut.*)

(*silence*)

IONE:

Oh, I'm proud of you.

MCGAFFERTY:

Ione! Here still?

IONE:

Hidden in this leather chair.
No one saw me. You were wonderful.

MCGAFFERTY:

Wonderful I don't think. I was voted down —
voted out — deposed — exterminated!

IONE:

And now you can come home with me.

MCGAFFERTY:

Come where?
You think the danger's past? The panic's over?

IONE:

I think it's night. I think it's late.
I think you need to sleep a little.
Nothing can happen now till morning.

Come home with me. I've laid a fire —
a pitch-pine knot and two logs, maple —
and after supper we can watch the shadows
flickering on the ceiling, that soft light.

MCGAFFERTY:
You know I can't. I have a thousand . . .

IONE:
Yes, but not till morning.

MCGAFFERTY:
                      There will
be no morning if I let them go.

IONE:
I can prophesy as well as you —
or any blind man. If you stay here
struggling with inevitable doom, the doom
will *be* inevitable — and for you!
Come home with me . . .

                      come home . . .

                              come home.

MCGAFFERTY:
Ah . . . You're right. I'm tired. Tired.

(*silence*)

Banks have closed before and still the sun rose . . .

IONE:
Come! The room's warm and so high the traffic
sounds like surf along an island shore.
We'll think of islands off in the Aegean . . .

(*the telephone — sharp, insistent*)

No! Don't answer it!

54

MCGAFFERTY:

McGafferty . . .

IONE:

Don't

answer!

MCGAFFERTY:

Any time tomorrow . . .

No, not

now . . .

tomorrow . . .

IONE:

Hurry! Please, please hurry.

MCGAFFERTY:

Shelton . . . ?

What did you say about Shelton?

Well,

ask him . . .

IONE:

No! Oh no! Oh no!

MCGAFFERTY:

Then send him up. I'll wait for him. Hurry!

(*Telephone is returned to its cradle: the dead sound.*)

Griggs. Of American. He's downstairs.
Something happened to Shelton. You know Shelton.
Ran American for years.
Best man on the Street. Not Griggs,
Griggs is an ass.

(*silence*)

(*stiffly*)

Sorry to keep you waiting.

55

IONE: (*artificial*)

Oh, it doesn't matter. I thought if we could . . .

(*Her voice breaks. A knock.*)

MCGAFFERTY:

Yes. Come in. Is that you, Griggs?

(*The door opens.*)

GRIGGS: (*thin, dry voice*)

Am I . . . intruding?

MCGAFFERTY:

No. Come in. Sit down.

GRIGGS:

But what I have to . . .

MCGAFFERTY:

Anything you have to . . .

GRIGGS:

What I have to say is . . . delicate.

IONE:

Shall I?

MCGAFFERTY:

Stay where you are. Go on, Griggs.

GRIGGS:

Shelton's dead.

IONE:

(*A cry — caught and stifled.*)

GRIGGS:

Shot himself . . . They called me.

MCGAFFERTY:

It's not true.

56

GRIGGS:
It's true enough. I saw him.

MCGAFFERTY:
                                It's not
true. He wouldn't. Couldn't. Let the rest
run for cover — dig themselves a hole — he
wouldn't. Men like that don't kill themselves.

GRIGGS:
I know.

MCGAFFERTY:
        He did though . . .

(*silence*)

                        How?

GRIGGS:
                        I told you —
shot himself. Look here, McGafferty:
let's omit the sentiments. We've made you
chairman. Oh, I know. I know.
You said you'd never take it. There's no choice.
Only your name can stop the run tomorrow.

MCGAFFERTY:
Where?

GRIGGS:
        Where what? Oh — Shelton. In the washroom.

MCGAFFERTY:
Dead in a urinal, the gray-haired man.
Greasy blood on the mopped marble . . .

GRIGGS:
I said, sir, we had made you chairman.
Will you serve? We have no time . . .

MCGAFFERTY:

No. We have no time. He learned that
standing there before those glaring
mirrors with his gun . . .

                               He learned it . . .

(*pause*)

He'd always thought our people on this continent
had all the time there was to live by:
found their great republic in the wilderness;
build their towering cities; shape the world.
Now there was no future: only fate.

(*pause*)

Our fathers forged their destiny themselves like
men . . .

                We take it, spoon-fed, from the prophets,
priests, who know the age of men is done,
the age of faceless masses is beginning . . .

(*pause*)

Necessity has murdered time . . .

(*pause*)

                            But why did
Shelton —
        Shelton!
                — lick that childish
pap from the soiled spoon? He'd heard the
oracles before and laughed.
Why shoot himself before a mirror?
Because the market had collapsed? He'd seen
collapsing markets over half a century.
Because the breadlines in the snow were longer?

The banks were closing? Factories shut down?
All that had happened long before . . .

(*pause*)

What did he know that we don't? . . .

(*pause*)

                                           I don't?

GRIGGS:
Are you saying yes or no?

IONE:
                         He's saying
No! You have no right to . . .

MCGAFFERTY:
                             Yes.
I'll serve as chairman. Call the papers.

GRIGGS: (*Chair is pushed back.*)
You'll be hearing from me before midnight.
Thanks . . .

(*The door opens: the ticker is louder.*)

                       Good night!

(*The door slams shut: the ticker is muted.*)

IONE:
                       Thank *you*! . . .

(*Silence: she laughs — tries to.*)

You said . . . but that was long ago.
Hours ago. Eons anyway. You said
I would not love you when the world came down.
And now the world's come down. And now it's
you who . . .

MCGAFFERTY:

What?

IONE:

Won't.

(*pause*)

You said you'd
come with me. You didn't. Now you'll
stay here in this haunted room
the telephone beside you — someone
waiting for you . . .

in a mirror.

MCGAFFERTY:

No!

IONE:
Yes!

(*pause*)

Oh, my dear love, my love, you've left me.
You think you know what Shelton knew — that there is
nothing any man on earth can
do to overcome his destiny.
You mean to face disaster where he faced it —
not in the street, the city, the Republic —
not in the waking world where it might end
but in the mirror where he'd end it for himself.

MCGAFFERTY:
Not Shelton!

IONE:

You then?

60

(*silence*)

> And I think that love
has no part left to play in this for you.

MCGAFFERTY:
In what?

IONE:

> In what you mean to do.
> > How can it?

MCGAFFERTY:
What I mean to do is run these banks.
You don't run banks in times like these for love.

IONE:
Even in times like these a woman,
living in an agony of fear,
can love the man she fears for. Do you
think of *her*? Does *she* concern you?

MCGAFFERTY:

> *Love!*
An old man — licked — rejected by the others —
powerless — his last, true, honest friend
dead by his own hand. And she can *love* him?
Oh, not love, Ione. Kindness . . .

IONE:
Kindness! Can *I* be *kind* to *you*?

(*silence*)

I do not know if you are old. I know I
love you. Is it wrong in me to love you?
Unnatural in me?
> Oh, my dear!

61

MCGAFFERTY:
Forgive me. No. It's generous . . .

IONE:
I do not know you.
You're gone and when I call to you it's someone
else turns back to speak.

(*silence*)

I do not
know you . . .

(*Ione's steps across the floor. She opens the door and leaves it open. The news-ticker has fallen silent, an occasional stitch of sound. The rest of the machines are mute. The room sounds empty as her footsteps cross it — fade. Silence.*)

MCGAFFERTY:
Ione!

(*We hear his footsteps. He calls after her*)

Ione!

(*silence*)

(*The telephone rings, urgent, clamoring. It goes on and on. Steps across the floor. The sound of a heavy window opening — wrenched open. The hum of wind in the room — the empty sound of wind. A long, long silence.*)

(*And then, abruptly, suddenly, the ticker — a frantic clatter. Heavy footsteps running — a watchman perhaps, a cleaning woman.*)

WATCHMAN:
What is it saying?

CLEANING WOMAN:
McGafferty . . .

WATCHMAN:

What about . . . ?

CLEANING WOMAN:
God knows! I can't make out. He's
dead . . .

WATCHMAN:
Dead!

CLEANING WOMAN:
He fell from a window . . .

WATCHMAN:
How could he fall from a window? There isn't a . . .

CLEANING WOMAN:
Oh, oh, I hear the wind!

WATCHMAN:
There isn't a window open anywhere I tell you . . .

CLEANING WOMAN:
No, but the wind . . .

THE END

The Fall of the City

Preface

It took my generation of Americans two world wars to learn that
an age had ended. When we went to the First World War in
1917 we believed in everything — in the war itself, in the Declaration of American Independence, in the revolution of mankind
which that Declaration announced.

I remember an apple orchard above the Marne on a summer
afternoon in 1918 and two New Mexico National Guardsmen,
shuffling their feet in the long grass. They wanted to know why
we were there — meaning by "there," not the orchard, but the
Second Battle of the Marne.

I reminded them of President Wilson's words, "to make the
world safe for democracy," and they nodded and walked off.
They knew, and I knew, that democracy, the right to think as
you pleased and say what you thought and govern yourself, was
what every human being wanted — the one cause worth dying
for in any country.

But twenty years later, when the Second World War was
about to begin, no one would have used Mr. Wilson's words to
answer that tragic question. Too many nations had walked away
from freedom by that time and accepted tyranny in its place —
Lenin's tyranny first . . . Mussolini's . . . Hitler's. And even in
the United States the double talk of those who had lost heart

had taken the place of Jefferson's honest English. "America first" meant, not that the old American commitment to human liberty came first, but that it didn't.

Our noble task was not to liberate France, which was already falling to Hitler, or to support Great Britain, which was near the end of its rope, but to look out for ourselves. And as for the rest of the world, if it preferred to live in police states rather than to persist in "the long labor of liberty," it was no concern of ours.

A courageous president and a magnificent army put an end to talk like that but we had glimpsed disaster and it was evident, even after we began to fight, that the great cause on which the Republic was founded was not a cause in which all mankind — even all Americans — believed. There were many who, left to themselves, would invent their conquerors and invite oppression as a way of life.

It was in the months of that realization that I wrote this play, using the everywhere of radio as a stage and all of history as a time — the imagined city of Tenochtitlán where, before Cortez conquered it, the dead woman appeared at noon at the tomb's door to prophecy: "The city of masterless men will take a master . . ."

I called it *The Fall of the City* and CBS produced it at the Seventh Regiment Armory in New York at seven o'clock on the evening of the eleventh of April, 1937, with Orson Welles, fresh from his actor's apprenticeship at the Gate Theatre in Dublin, as the Announcer and a crowd of high school students from New Jersey to fill the vast imagined square. It was, I have been told, the first verse play written for radio, but nobody knows how many listened to it — only that it was broadcast again a few months later from the Hollywood Bowl. But by that time Chamberlain had gone to Germany and returned with "peace in our time" and the city had fallen . . . not to be raised again until the greatest of all wars was won.

A. MacL.

THE VOICE OF THE STUDIO DIRECTOR: (*orotund, profes-sional*)
    Ladies and gentlemen:
    This broadcast comes to you from the city.
    Listeners over the curving air have heard
    From furthest-off frontiers of foreign hours —
    Mountain Time: Ocean Time: of the islands:
    Of waters after the islands — some of them waking
    Where noon here is the night there: some
    Where noon is the first few stars they see or the last one.

    For three days the world has watched this city —
    Not for the common occasions of brutal crime
    Or the usual violence of one sort or another
    Or coronations of kings or popular festivals:
    No: for stranger and disturbing reasons —
    The resurrection from death and the tomb of a dead woman.

    Each day for three days there has come
    To the door of her tomb at noon a woman buried!

    The terror that stands at the shoulder of our time
    Touches the cheek with this: the flesh winces.
    There have been other omens in other cities
    But never of this sort and never so credible.

In a time like ours seemings and portents signify.
Ours is a generation when dogs howl and the
Skin crawls on the skull with its beast's foreboding.
All men now alive with us have feared.
We have smelled the wind in the street that changes weather.
We have seen the familiar room grow unfamiliar:
The order of numbers alter: the expectation
Cheat the expectant eye. The appearance defaults with us.

Here in this city the wall of the time cracks.

We take you now to the great square of this city . . .

(*The shuffle and hum of a vast patient crowd gradually rises:
swells: fills the background.*)

THE VOICE OF THE ANNOUNCER: (*matter-of-fact*)
    We are here on the central plaza.
    We are well off to the eastward edge.
    There is a kind of terrace over the crowd here.
    It is precisely four minutes to twelve.
    The crowd is enormous: there might be ten thousand:
    There might be more: the whole square is faces.
    Opposite over the roofs are the mountains.
    It is quite clear: there are birds circling.
    We think they are kites by the look: they are very high . . .

    The tomb is off to the right somewhere —
    We can't see for the great crowd.
    Close to us here are the cabinet ministers:
    They stand on a raised platform with awnings.
    The farmers' wives are squatting on the stones:
    Their children have fallen asleep on their shoulders.
    The heat is harsh: the light dazzles like metal.
    It dazes the air as the clang of a gong does . . .

News travels in this nation:
There are people here from away off —
Horse-raisers out of the country with brooks in it:
Herders of cattle from up where the snow stays —
The kind that cook for themselves mostly:
They look at the girls with their eyes hard
And a hard grin and their teeth showing . . .

It is one minute to twelve now:
There is still no sign: they are still waiting:
No one doubts that she will come:
No one doubts that she will speak too:
Three times she has not spoken.

(*The murmur of the crowd changes — not louder but more
intense: higher.*)

THE VOICE OF THE ANNOUNCER: (*low but with increasing
    excitement*)
Now it is twelve: now they are rising:
Now the whole plaza is rising:
Fathers are lifting their small children:
The plumed fans on the platform are motionless . . .

There is no sound but the shuffle of shoe leather . . .

Now even the shoes are still . . .

We can hear the hawks: it is quiet as that now . . .

It is strange to see such throngs so silent . . .

Nothing yet: nothing has happened . . .

Wait! There's a stir here to the right of us:
They're turning their heads: the crowd turns:
The cabinet ministers lean from their balcony:
There's no sound: only the turning . . .

(A woman's voice comes over the silence of the crowd: it is a weak voice but penetrating: it speaks slowly and as though with difficulty.)

THE VOICE OF THE DEAD WOMAN:
First the waters rose with no wind . . .

THE VOICE OF THE ANNOUNCER: (*whispering*)
Listen: that is she! She's speaking!

THE VOICE OF THE DEAD WOMAN:
Then the stones of the temple kindled
Without flame or tinder of maize leaves . . .

THE VOICE OF THE ANNOUNCER: (*whispering*)
They see her beyond us: the crowd sees her . . .

THE VOICE OF THE DEAD WOMAN:
Then there were cries in the night haze:
Words in a once-heard tongue: the air
Rustling above us as at dawn with herons.

Now it is I who must bring fear:
I who am four days dead: the tears
Still unshed for me — all of them: I
For whom a child still calls at nightfall.

Death is young in me to fear!
My dress is kept still in the press in my bedchamber:
No one has broken the dish of the dead woman.

Nevertheless I must speak painfully:
I am to stand here in the sun and speak:

(There is a pause. Then her voice comes again loud, mechanical, speaking as by rote.)

The city of masterless men
Will take a master.

There will be shouting then:
Blood after!

(*The crowd stirs. Her voice goes on weak and slow as before.*)

Do not ask what it means: I do not know:
Only sorrow and no hope for it.

THE VOICE OF THE ANNOUNCER:
She has gone . . . No, they are still looking.

THE VOICE OF THE DEAD WOMAN:
It is hard to return from the time past. I have come
In the dream we must learn to dream where the crumbling of
Time like the ash from a burnt string has
Stopped for me. For you the thread still burns:
You take the feathery ash upon your fingers.
You bring yourselves from the time past as it pleases you.

It is hard to return to the old nearness . . .

Harder to go again . . .

THE VOICE OF THE ANNOUNCER:
                              She is gone.
We know because the crowd is closing.
All we can see is the crowd closing.
We hear the releasing of held breath —
The weight shifting: the lifting of shoe leather.
The stillness is broken as surface of water is broken —
The sound circling from in outward.

(*The murmur of the crowd rises.*)

Small wonder they feel fear.
Before the murders of the famous kings —
Before imperial cities burned and fell —
The dead were said to show themselves and speak.

73

When dead men came disaster came. Presentiments
That let the living on their beds sleep on
Woke dead men out of death and gave them voices.
All ancient men in every nation knew this.

A VOICE OVER THE CROWD:
Masterless men . . .

A VOICE OVER THE CROWD:
When shall it be . . .

A VOICE OVER THE CROWD:
Masterless men
Will take a master . . .

A VOICE OVER THE CROWD:
What has she said to us . . .

A VOICE OVER THE CROWD:
When shall it be . . .

A VOICE OVER THE CROWD:
Masterless men
Will take a master.
Blood after . . .

A VOICE OVER THE CROWD:
What has she said to us . . .

VOICES TOGETHER:
Blood after!

(*The voices run together into the excited roar of the crowd.
The Announcer's voice is loud over it.*)

THE VOICE OF THE ANNOUNCER:
They are milling around us like cattle that smell death.
The whole square is whirling and turning and shouting.
One of the ministers raises his arms on the platform.

No one is listening: now they are sounding drums:
Trying to quiet them likely: No! No!
Something is happening: there in the far corner:
A runner: a messenger: staggering: people are helping him:
People are calling: he comes through the crowd: they are quieter.
Only those on the far edge are still shouting:
Listen! He's here by the ministers now! He is speaking . . .

THE VOICE OF THE MESSENGER:
There has come the conqueror!
I am to tell you.
I have raced over sea land:
I have run over cane land:
I have climbed over cone land.
It was laid on my shoulders
By shall and by shan't
That standing by day
And staying by night
Were not for my lot
Till I came to the sight of you.
Now I have come.

Be warned of this conqueror!
This one is dangerous!
Word has out-oared him.
East over sea-cross has
All taken —
Every country.
No men are free there.
Ears overhear them.
Their words are their murderers.
Judged before judgment
Tried after trial
They die as do animals: —

Offer their throats
As the goat to her slaughterer.
Terror has taught them this!

Now he is here!

He was violent in his vessel:
He was steering in her stern:
He was watching in her waist:
He was peering in her prow:
And he dragged her up
Nine lengths
Till her keel lodged
On this nation.

Now he is here
Waylaying and night-lying.
If they hide before dark
He comes before sunup.
Where hunger is eaten
There he sits down:
Where fear sleeps
There he arises.

I tell you beware of him!
All doors are dangers.
The warders of wealth
Will admit him by stealth.
The lovers of men
Will invite him as friend.
The drinkers of blood
Will drum him in suddenly.
Hope will unlatch to him:
Hopelessness open.

I say and say truly
To all men in honesty

Such is this conqueror!
Shame is his people. .
Lickers of spittle
Their lives are unspeakable:
Their dying indecent.

Be well warned!
He comes to you slightly
Slanting and sprinting
Hinting and shadowing:
Sly is his hiding: —
A hard lot:
A late rider:

Watch! I have said to you!

THE VOICE OF THE ANNOUNCER:
    They are leading him out: his legs give:
    Now he is gone in the crowd: they are silent:
    No one has spoken since his speaking:

    They stand still circling the ministers.
    No one has spoken or called out: —
    There is no stir at all nor movement:
    Even the farthest have stood patiently:
    They wait trusting the old men:
    They wait faithfully trusting the answer.
    Now the huddle on the platform opens:
    A minister turns to them raising his two arms . . .

THE VOICE OF THE ORATOR:
    Freemen of this nation!
    The persuasion of your wills against your wisdom is not
        dreamed of.
    We offer themes for your consideration.

77

What is the surest defender of liberty?
Is it not liberty?

A free people resists by freedom:
Not locks! Not blockhouses!

The future is a mirror where the past
Marches to meet itself. Go armed toward arms!
Peaceful toward peace! Free and with music toward freedom!
Face tomorrow with knives and tomorrow's a knife-blade.
Murder your foe and your foe will be murder! —
Even your friends suspected of false-speaking:
Hands on the door at night and the floorboards squeaking.

Those who win by the spear are the spear-toters.
And what do they win? Spears! What else is there?
If their hands let go they have nothing to hold by.
They are no more free than a paralytic propped against a tree
    is.

With the armored man the arm is upheld by the weapon:
The man is worn by the knife.

Once depend on iron for your freedom and your
Freedom's iron!
Once overcome your resisters with force and your
Force will resist you! —
You will never be free of force.
Never of arms unarmed
Will the father return home:
The lover to her loved:
The mature man to his fruit orchard
Walking at peace in that beauty —
The years of his trees to assure him.

Force is a greater enemy than this conqueror —
A treacherous weapon.

Nevertheless my friends there *is* a weapon!
Weakness conquers!

Against chainlessness who breaks?
Against wall-lessness who vaults?
Against forcelessness who forces?

Against the feather of the thistle
Is blunted sharpest metal.
No edge cuts seed-fluff.

This conqueror unresisted
Will conquer no longer: a posturer
Beating his blows upon burdocks —
Shifting his guard against shadows.
Snickers will sound among road-menders:
Titters be stifled by laundresses:
Coarse guffaws among chambermaids.
Reddened with rage he will roar.
He will sweat in his uniform foolishly.
He will disappear: no one hear of him!

There *is* a weapon my friends.
Scorn conquers!

THE VOICE OF THE ANNOUNCER: (*the Orator's voice unin-
    telligible under it*)
I wish you could all see this as we do —
The whole plaza full of these people —
Their colorful garments — the harsh sunlight —
The water-sellers swinging enormous gourds —
The orator there on the stone platform —
The temple behind him: the high pyramid —
The hawks overhead in the sky teetering
Slow to the windward: swift to the downwind —
The houses blind with the blank sun on them . . .

THE VOICE OF THE ORATOR:
   There is a weapon.
   Reason and truth are that weapon.

   Let this conqueror come!
   Show him no hindrance!
   Suffer his flag and his drum!
   Words . . . win!

THE VOICE OF THE ANNOUNCER:
   There's the shout now: he's done:
   He's climbing down: a great speech:
   They're all smiling and pressing around him:
   The women are squatting in full sunlight:
   They're opening packages: bread we'd say by the look —
   Yes: bread: bread wrapped between corn leaves:
   They're squatting to eat: they're quite contented and happy:
   Women are calling their men from the sunny stones:
   There are flutes sounding away off:
   We can't see for the shifting and moving —
   Yes: there are flutes in the cool shadow:
   Children are dancing in intricate figures.

   (A *drum and flute are heard under the voice.*)

   Even a few old men are dancing.
   You'd say they'd never feared to see them dancing.
   A great speech! really great!
   Men forget these truths in passion:
   They oppose the oppressors with blind blows:
   They make of their towns tombs: of their roofs burials:
   They build memorial ruins to liberty:
   But liberty is not built from ruins:
   Only in peace is the work excellent . . .

   That's odd! The music has stopped. There's something —
   It's a man there on the far side: he's pointing:

80

He seems to be pointing back through the farthest street:
The people are twisting and rising: bread in their fists . . .
We can't see what it is . . . Wait! . . . it's a messenger.
It must be a messenger. Yes. It's a message — another.
Here he is at the turn of the street trotting:
His neck's back at the nape: he looks tired:
He winds through the crowd with his mouth open: laboring:
People are offering water: he pushes away from them:
Now he has come to the stone steps: to the ministers:
Stand by: we're edging in . . .

(*There are sounds of people close by: coughs: murmurs. The
Announcer's voice is lowered.*)

Listen: he's leaning on the stone: he's speaking.

THE VOICE OF THE MESSENGER:
There has come . . . the conqueror . . .

I am to tell you . . .

I have run over corn land:
I have climbed over cone land:
I have crossed over mountains . . .

It was laid on my shoulders
By shall and by shan't
That standing by day
And staying by night
Were not for my lot
Till I came to the sight of you . . .

Now I have come.

I bear word:
Beware of this conqueror!

The fame of his story
Like flame in the winter grass

81

Widens before him.
Beached on our shore
With the dawn over shoulder
The lawns were still cold
When he came to the sheep meadows: —
Sun could not keep with him
So was he forward.

Fame is his sword.

No man opposing him
Still grows his glory.
He needs neither foeman nor
Thickset of blows to
Gather his victories —
Nor a foe's match
To earn him his battles.

He brings his own enemy!

He baggages with him
His closet antagonist —
His private opposer.
He's setting him up
At every road corner —
A figure of horror
With blood for his color:
Fist for his hand:
Reek where he stands:
Hate for his heat:
Sneers for his mouth:
Clouts for his clothes:
Oaths if he speak: —
And he's knocking him down
In every town square
Till hair's on his blade

And blood's all about
Like dust in a drouth
And the people are shouting
Flowers him flinging
Music him singing
And bringing him gold
And holding his heels
And feeling his thighs
Till their eyes start
And their hearts swell
And they're telling his praises
Like lays of the heroes
And chiefs of antiquity.

Such are his victories!
So does he come:
So he approaches . . .

(A *whisper rustles through the crowd.*)

No man to conquer
Yet as a conqueror
Marches he forward . . .

(*The whisper is louder.*)

Stands in your mountains . . .

(A *murmur of voices.*)

Soon to descend on you!

(A *swelling roar.*)

THE VOICE OF THE ANNOUNCER:
That touched them! That frightened them!
Some of them point to the east hills:
Some of them mock at the ministers: "Freedom!"
"Freedom for what? To die in a rat trap?"

83

They're frantic with anger and plain fear.
They're sold out they say. You can hear them.
"Down with the government! Down with the orators!
"Down with liberal learned minds!
"Down with the mouths and the loose tongues in them!
"Down with the lazy lot! They've sold us!
"We're sold out! Talking has done for us!"
They're boiling around us like mullet that smell shark.
We can't move for the mob: they're crazy with terror . . .

A LOUD VOICE: (*distant*)
    God-lovers!
    Think of your gods!

    Earth-masters!
    Taste your disasters!

    Men!
    Remember!

THE VOICE OF THE ANNOUNCER:
    There's a voice over the crowd somewhere.
    They hear it: they're quieting down . . . It's the priests!
    We see them now: it's the priests on the pyramid!
    There might be ten of them: black with their hair tangled.
    The smoke of their fire is flat in the quick wind:
    They stand in the thick of the smoke by the stone of the
        victims:
    Their knives catch in the steep sun: they are shouting:
    Listen! —

VOICES OF THE PRIESTS:
    Turn to your gods rememberers!

A SINGLE VOICE:
    Let the world be saved by surrendering the world:
        Not otherwise shall it be saved.

84

VOICES OF THE PRIESTS:
  Turn to your gods rememberers!

A SINGLE VOICE:
  Let evil be overcome by the coming over of evil:
    Your hearts shall be elsewhere.

VOICES OF THE PRIESTS:
  Turn to your gods rememberers!

VOICES OF THE PRIESTS: (*antiphonally*)
  Turn to your gods!
    The conqueror cannot take you!

  Turn to your gods!
    The narrow dark will keep you!

  Turn to your gods!
    In god's house is no breaking!

  Turn to your gods!
    In god's silences sleep is!

  Lay up your will with the gods!
    Stones cannot still you!

  Lay up your mind with the gods!
    Blade cannot blind you!

  Lay up your heart with the gods!
    Danger departs from you!

THE VOICE OF THE ANNOUNCER:
  It's a wonderful thing to see this crowd responding.
  Even the simplest citizens feel the emotion.
  There's hardly a sound now in the square. It's wonderful:
  Really impressive: the priests there on the pyramid:
  The smoke blowing: the bright sun: the faces —

85

A SINGLE VOICE:
   In the day of confusion of reason when all is delusion:
   In the day of the tyrants of tongues when the truth is for hire:
   In the day of deceit when ends meet:
   Turn to your gods!

   In the day of division of nations when hope is derision:
   In the day of the supping of hate when the soul is corrupted:
   In the day of despair when the heart's bare:
   Turn to your gods!

   (A *slow drum beat.*)

THE VOICE OF THE ANNOUNCER:
   A kind of dance is beginning: a serpent of people:
   A current of people coiling and curling through people:
   A circling of people through people like water through
      water . . .

CHANTING VOICES: (*to the drums*)
   Out of the stir of the sun
   Out of the shout of the thunder
   Out of the hush of the star . . .
   Withdraw the heart.

THE VOICE OF THE ANNOUNCER: (*the chant and drums
      under*)
   A very young girl is leading them:
   They have torn the shawl from her bare breast:
   They are giving her flowers: her mouth laughs:
   Her eyes are not laughing . . .

CHANTING VOICES:
   Leave now the lovely air
   To the sword and the sword-wearer —
   Leave to the marksman the mark —
   Withdraw the heart.

86

THE VOICE OF THE ANNOUNCER: (*the chant and drums louder*)
> She's coming . . . the drums pound . . . the crowd
> Shrieks . . . she's reaching the temple . . . she's climbing
>   it . . .
> Others are following: five: ten . . .
> Hundreds are following . . . crowding the stairway . . .
> She's almost there . . . her flowers have fallen . . .
> She looks back . . . the priests are surrounding her . . .

(*The drums suddenly stop: there is an instant's silence: then an angry shout from the crowd.*)

THE VOICE OF THE ANNOUNCER:
> Wait! Wait! Something has happened!
> One of the ministers: one of the oldest:
> The general: the one in the feathered coat: —
> He's driving them down with the staff of a banner:
> He's climbed after them driving them down:
> There's shouting and yelling enough but they're going:
> He's telling them off too: you can hear him —

A DEEP VOICE: (*chatter of the crowd under it*)
> Men! Old men! Listen!
> Twist your necks on your nape bones!
> The knife will wait in the fist for you.
> There is a time for everything —
> Time to be thinking of heaven:
> Time of your own skins!

> Cock your eyes to the windward!

> Do you see smoke on those mountains?
> The smoke is the smoke of towns.
> And who makes it? The conqueror!
> And where will he march now? Onward!
> The heel of the future descends on you!

THE VOICE OF THE ANNOUNCER:
He has them now: even the priests have seen it:
They're all looking away here to the east.
There's smoke too: filling the valleys: like thunderheads!

THE VOICE OF THE GENERAL:
You are foolish old men.

You ought to be flogged for your foolishness.
Your grandfathers died to be free
And you — you juggle with freedom!
Do you think you're free by a law
Like the falling of apples in autumn?

You thought you were safe in your liberties!
You thought you could always quibble!
You can't! You take my word for it.
Freedom's the rarest bird!
You risk your neck to snare it —
It's gone while your eyeballs stare!

Those who'd lodge with a tyrant
Thinking to feed at his fire
And leave him again when they're fed are
Plain fools or were bred to it —
Brood of the servile races
Born with the hangdog face . . .

THE VOICE OF THE ANNOUNCER:
They're all pointing and pushing together:
The women are shouldering baskets: bread: children . . .
They smell smoke in the air: they smell terror . . .

THE VOICE OF THE GENERAL: (*louder over the increasing sound*)
There's nothing in this world worse —
Empty belly or purse or the

Pitiful hunger of children —
Than doing the Strong Man's will!

The free will fight for their freedom.
They're free men first. They feed
Meager or fat but as free men.
Everything else comes after —
Food: roof: craft —
Even the sky and the light of it!

(*The voices of the crowd rise to a tumult of sounds — drums: shouts: cries.*)

THE VOICE OF THE ANNOUNCER:
  The sun is yellow with smoke . . . the town's burning . . .
  The war's at the broken bridge . . .

THE VOICE OF THE GENERAL: (*shouting*)
  You! Are you free? Will you fight?

  There are still inches for fighting!

  There is still a niche in the streets!

  You can stand on the stairs and meet him!

  You can hold in the dark of a hall!

  You can die!

    — or your children will crawl for it!

THE VOICE OF THE ANNOUNCER: (*over the tumult*)
  They won't listen. They're shouting and screaming and
    circling.
  The square is full of deserters with more coming.
  Every street from the bridge is full of deserters.
  They're rolling in with the smoke blowing behind them.
  The plaza's choked with the smoke and the struggling of
    stragglers.

They're climbing the platform: driving the ministers: shout-
    ing —
One speaks and another:

THE VOICES OF CITIZENS:
    The city is doomed!
                    There's no holding it!

    Let the conqueror have it! It's his!

    The age is his! It's his century!

    Our institutions are obsolete.
    He marches a mile while we sit in a meeting.

    Opinions and talk!
    Deliberative walks beneath the ivy and the creepers!

    The age demands a made-up mind.
    The conqueror's mind is decided on everything.

    His doubt comes after the deed or never.

    He knows what he wants for his want's what he knows.
    He's gone before they say he's going.
    He's come before you've barred your house.

    He's one man: we are but thousands!

    Who can defend us from one man?

    Bury your arms! Break your standards!

    Give him the town while the town stands!

THE VOICE OF THE ANNOUNCER:
    They're throwing their arms away: their bows are in bonfires.
    The plaza is littered with torn plumes: spear-handles . . .

THE VOICES OF CITIZENS:
    Masterless men!

Masterless men
Must take a master!

Order must master us!

Freedom's for fools:
Force is the certainty!

Freedom has eaten our strength and corrupted our virtues!

Men must be ruled!

Fools must be mastered!

Rigor and fast
Will restore us our dignity!

Chains will be liberty!

THE VOICE OF THE ANNOUNCER:
The last defenders are coming: they whirl from the streets like
Wild leaves on a wind: the square scatters them.

Now they are fewer — ten together or five:
They come with their heads turned: their eyes back.

Now there are none. The street's empty — in shadow.
The crowd is retreating — watching the empty street:
The shouts die.

The voices are silent.

They're watching . . .

They stand in the slant of the sunlight silent and watching.
The silence after the drums echoes the drum beat.

Now there's a sound. They see him. They must see him!
They're shading their eyes from the sun: there's a rustle of
    whispering:
We can't see for the glare of it . . . Yes! . . . Yes! . . .

He's there in the end of the street in the shadow. We see him!
He looks huge — a head taller than anyone:
Broad as a brass door: a hard hero:
Heavy of heel on the brick: clanking with metal:
The helm closed on his head: the eyeholes hollow.

He's coming! . . .
                    He's clear of the shadow! . . .
                                        The sun takes him.

They cover their faces with fingers. They cower before him.
They fall: they sprawl on the stone. He's alone where he's
    walking.
He marches with rattle of metal. He tramples his shadow.
He mounts by the pyramid — stamps on the stairway —
    turns —
His arm rises — his visor is opening . . .

(*There is an instant's breathless silence: then the voice of the
Announcer low — almost a whisper.*)

                                    There's no one! . . .
There's no one at all! . . .
                    No one! . . .
                                    The helmet is hollow!
The metal is empty! The armor is empty! I tell you
There's no one at all there: there's only the metal:
The barrel of metal: the bundle of armor. It's empty!

The push of a stiff pole at the nipple would topple it.

They don't see! They lie on the paving. They lie in the
Burnt spears: the ashes of arrows. They lie there . . .
They don't see or they won't see. They are silent . . .

The people invent their oppressors: they wish to believe in
    them.

They wish to be free of their freedom: released from their
   liberty: —
The long labor of liberty ended!
                              They lie there!

*(There is a whisper of sound. The Announcer's voice is
louder.)*

Look! It's his arm! It is rising! His arm's rising!
They're watching his arm as it rises. They stir. They cry.
They cry out. They are shouting. They're shouting with hap-
   piness.
Listen! They're shouting like troops in a victory. Listen —
"The city of masterless men has found a master!"
You'd say it was they were the conquerors: they that had con-
   quered.

A ROAR OF VOICES:
   The city of masterless men has found a master!
   The city has fallen!
   The city has fallen!

THE VOICE OF THE ANNOUNCER: *(flat)*
   The city has fallen . . .

                    THE END

                       93

Air Raid

Preface

Air Raid was written in the summer of 1938 — finished a few weeks before Chamberlain went to Munich. But it was not the blundering of the diplomats in that fatal summer which gave the play its theme. Rather it was something that had happened the year before in the Basque town of Guernica and on a canvas of Picasso's.

Picasso had been asked by the Spanish government to paint a mural for its exhibit at the 1937 Paris world's fair, and on the twenty-eighth of April that year German planes, using the Spanish Civil War as practice ground for the Nazi conquest of Europe already planned, bombed the undefended city of Guernica without warning or even declaration of war. On May first Picasso began his picture, perhaps the greatest — certainly the most famous — painting of the century. Its name, too, was *Guernica*, and though critics have complained that its painter never provided an "exact explanation" of its content there can be few living men or women — particularly women — who cannot bring its images to mind: the dead child and the shrieking woman, the kneeling woman, the running woman, the stabbed horse, the shattered soldier, the arrogant triumphant bull.

Guernica is not a political protest. It is a work of art. A work of art which *sees*. And what it sees is a new world — a new world of war. A new and unspeakable horror of war. A war waged not by armies against armies but by machines in the blind sky against cities, against the women and children of open cities. That lamp thrust in by an arm from elsewhere to the center of the screaming picture is the lamp of art that sees and shows. With the painting of *Guernica* the inhumanity of man saw its human horror.

I no longer remember where or how I first came face to face with *Guernica* — probably that same year in a reproduction in a newspaper. I only know that when I saw it first, I *heard* it — began to hear it: the women's voices at their work, the calling children, the radio crew on the roofs somewhere watching the sky to the northeast, the scene with which the play begins.

A. MacL.

VOICE:
> When you hear the gong sound . . .
> The time will be . . .
> Ten seconds past two A.M. precisely . . .

> (*gong signal*)

VOICE:
> WABC . . . New York . . .

STUDIO DIRECTOR:
> Ladies and gentlemen:
> You have only one thought tonight all of you
>
> You who fish the fathoms of the night
> With poles on rooftops and long loops of wire
>
> Those of you who driving from some visit
> Finger the button on the dashboard dial
> Until the metal trembles like a medium in a trance
> And tells you what is happening in France
> Or China or in Spain or some such country
> You have one thought tonight and only one:
> Will there be war? Has war come?
> Is Europe burning from the Tiber to the Somme?
>
> You think you hear the sudden double thudding of the drum

You don't though . . .

> Not now . . .

But what your ears will hear within the hour
No one living in this world would try to tell you.
We take you there to wait it for yourselves.

Stand by: we'll try to take you through . . .

(*The station cuts out: there is a moment's delay: it cuts in again.*)

STUDIO DIRECTOR:
One moment now: we'll try to take you.

The ultimatum you remember was for sunrise by their clock:
Midnight by ours. Now ours is long past midnight.

The sun is up on the whole curve of that continent.

The weather is fair with winds southwest going southerly:
A few clouds at ten thousand — cumulus:
Mists among the passes of the upper Julian Alps:
Some fog on the east Baltic but lifting:

Otherwise sun: the Tyrrhenian Sea all sunshine:
The Adriatic creased with curling light.

The Atlantic tumbles forward into morning on those beaches.

The whole continent lolls in summer sunlight:
Spain is drifting eastward with the shapes of clouds:
France is smooth with morning as a turf:
Germany is checkered with the squares of green and grain:

The visibility is perfect . . .

You think you hear the lonely droning danger of the planes

You don't though . . .

> Not yet . . .

(The station cuts out: cuts in again.)

STUDIO DIRECTOR:
  One moment now we'll take you through.

  We take you to a town behind the border —
  One of those old-time hill-towns where the papers
  Come tomorrow morning and the wars
  Come years ago or in some other country:

  The planes will come though — if they come at all:

  The pass above the border is to eastward in those mountains.

  Our men are on a roof above the houses of the town.

  Strange and curious times these times we live in:
  You watch from kitchens for the bloody signs:
  You watch for breaking war above the washing on the lines.

  In the old days they watched along the borders:
  They called their warfare in the old days wars
  And fought with men and men who fought were killed:

  We call it peace and kill the women and the children.

  Our women die in peace beneath the lintels of their doors.

  We have learned much: civilization has gentled us:
  We have learned to take the dying and the wounds without
    the wars.

  Stand by please: we take you through now . . .

  *(The "note" of the station changes: the Studio Director's
  voice falls away as he speaks. At the end it is almost lost.)*

  We take you now across the traveler's sea

  Across the trawler's coast

                    the parson's orchard

101

Across the merchant's villa with the vine above the porch

Across the laborer's city with the flames above the forges

Across the drover's plain

                    the planter's valley . . .

The poplar trees in alleys are the roads

The linden trees in couples are the doors

The willows are the wandering water flowing

The pines in double lines are where the north wind burns the
    orchards

Those are the mountains where no meadow is squared nor a
Stream straight: nor a road: nor water quiet

The town is in those mountains: you are there

(*The station cuts out: we hear the undefined murmur and
clatter and laughing of a waking town on a fine summer
day.*)

THE ANNOUNCER: (*flat: dry*)
    You are twenty-eight miles from the eastern border:
    You are up on top of a town on a kind of tenement:
    You are out the other side the night —
    The sun dazzles you: not the lightbulb.
    You are staring out to eastward toward the sun.

    We have seen nothing and heard nothing:
    Before dawn we thought we heard them:
    It was wind we heard in the valley cedars.

    Sounds rise to this roof —
    Hoofs of stabled horses: leaves:
    Even the speaking of sleepers rises.

Many sleep in the one house here:
They work in the fields: sleep in the village:
The men go out at dawn: return
To evening burning from the chimneys:
The women keep the town between.

(*Under the Announcer's voice the voices of women have been
rising: gay: laughing: the words indistinguishable.*)

They keep it now: the tenement's full of them —
A four-story building of women:
They're filling the court with their quick talk:
They call back and forth from the windows:
They laugh behind the kitchen doors:
They rinse the shirts in the first real shine of the morning:
They talk — their arms to elbows in the tubs —

WOMEN'S VOICES:
Who did she say?

        When did she say so? . . .

                . . . Look at it!
Look at the cuff on his shirt! What's he been into?
Black grease!

        What would you think he'd be into —
A man like yours with an eye like his for wandering.

And you to talk! — you with that red-headed lollypop!
Hardly a day at dark but his head's in the window.

He's wearing his elbows out on the stone sill
Looking us over from one floor to the next:
If it's only the eye with him that wanders I wonder . . .

THE OLD WOMAN'S VOICE:
A fine day I told him: a fine day:
A fine willing day: he could trust it for certain:

He could hay today and cock it tomorrow for certain.
Ah those arctic stars, he said . . .

A BOY'S VOICE: (*calling*)
                              Harry!
Harry! Be quick Harry! Be quick! Quick!

AN OLD WOMAN'S VOICE:
Men are the fools: they have no trust in the world:
To make a crop of hay you're bound to trust it:
There's no sin but not to trust the world.

GIRLS' VOICES:
When will she marry?

                    She won't marry:
He's always planning for something or other:
He's always fearing or hoping or something.

They never seem to know it's now —
Men don't: women sometimes do.

They're always waiting for the time
They've waited for.

                    And when it comes

They still wait.

                    Don't they?

                              But they do.
They never take the clock for *now* —
For *this* — for *here*. They never take the
Risk that this was why they waited.

Men don't: women sometimes do.

No: not sometimes: always do.

Life's more like itself for us than
Them. They're always meddling with it —
Always making life come true . . .

(*Over the laughter and the voices a woman's voice, very high
and clear and pure, singing a scale — Ah! Ah! Ah! Ah! . . .*)

WOMEN'S VOICES:
It's war again! Have you heard them talking?

                                        We've heard them.
How can we help but hear them — blabbing about:
Cocking their feet on the kitchen table and talking.

It's always war when they talk and it's always talk.

It's always talk when they get to the beer and tobacco.

The beer comes out of the bottles: the talk too.

Yes and the wars!

                    Wasting their time on wars with the
Dishes to do and the children to chasten.

                                    The wars!
As though to make the wars were something wonderful!
Millions of men have made the wars and talked.

Talking of wars as though to die were something!

Death's the one thing every creature does
And none does well I've ever seen — the one thing
Weak and foolish every creature does.

Only boys and men like boys believe in it.

It's sticking to this giddy world that's hard —
Not turning limp and letting loose and tumbling.

105

THE BOY'S VOICE:
   Harry! Harry! Harry! Be quick Harry!

GIRLS' VOICES:
   Ah the petticoat! Look at the petticoat, Maudie!
   Look at the petticoat will you! Isn't it hers?

   Who would wear it but her? But who? — who?

   Who but my mother!

                    Who but her mother!

   (*The girls' voices pick up a chanting beat which works into a kind of tuneless tune.*)

   Who but her mother and where will she wear it to?

   Who will she show it to?

                         Where will she go in it?

   Where will she go in the silk of her petticoat?

   Who will she show the silk in her petticoat?

   How would he know it was silk in her petticoat?

   How would he know?

                    How would he know . . .

   (*There is a shriek of laughter. The chant and the words are repeated indistinguishably under the Announcer's voice. They fade to a murmur of voices.*)

THE ANNOUNCER:
   We have seen nothing and heard nothing.
   If they left at dawn we should have heard them.
   It's two hours now since dawn.
   They could make it in two: they could make it under —
   One and a half from their fields to the border:
   Ten minutes more . . .

(A tinny piano begins far off — a few indistinguishable phrases of summer morning music.)

We have seen
Nothing at all. We have heard nothing.
The town is very quiet and orderly.
They are flushing the cobblestones with water.
The sidewalks are slippery with sun.
It smells of a summer morning anywhere:
It smells of seven o'clock in the morning in
Any town they water dust in.
Towns are all the same in summer.
A man can remember the name of his own in
Any city after the water carts.

(The Singing Woman's voice rises again in the high, pure scale.)

The last shutters are opening —
The rooms where no one hopes: the rooms
Where all the hope's been had and sleep
Covers it: folding it. Rooms where the old lie:
Rooms where the young lie late with their lovers . . .

A SICK WOMAN'S VOICE: *(close: weak: wandering)*
How much longer must I wait? They've told you.

A BOY'S VOICE:
Wait for what mother? Wait to be well?

THE SICK WOMAN'S VOICE:
Wait to be . . . Yes. Not long . . . A day is long . . .
It's always long the first time . . . I remember
Someone saying it was always long . . .
Someone saying it will come: don't fear it . . .

THE BOY'S VOICE:
Were you never afraid mother?

THE SICK WOMAN'S VOICE:
                              Never: of anything.
   There's nothing comes by day or night to fear.

THE BOY'S VOICE:
   Not even war? Not even if they came here?

THE SICK WOMAN'S VOICE:
   They came when I was young once: I remember them.
   We smelled the smoke one morning in the alders . . .
   They had their tents by the stream in the water meadow . . .
   I'd never eat the sausages . . . I was the dainty one:
   I used to rinse my things in seven waters —
   Well-water: brook-water: rain . . .
   I dried them on the gravel by the river.
   Even at night late they would smell of the sun on them . . .
   I ate the watercress to make my mouth sweet . . .
   They had blue capes on their coats with scarlet linings:
   They spoke together in another tongue:
   They were slow and soft in their speech with laughter and
      looking . . .
   Evenings coming home across the evening:
   Seeing the constellations of the stars:
   They gave us milk to drink from jars of metal . . .

   You sit in the dark and drink: you don't say anything . . .

THE BOY'S VOICE:
   They kill the children when they come. I've read it.

THE SICK WOMAN'S VOICE:
   Not "It's a pleasant night." Not even "Thank you."
   They seem to want you not to speak or move:
   They seem to want you quiet like the heifers.
   You sit in the dark and rest: you don't say anything . . .
   You don't say "Thank you" even . . . not "Good night."

THE BOY'S VOICE:
I've heard they kill the children, mother! I've heard it.
I've heard at night in sleep they kill the children!

(*Under the close voices of the Sick Woman and the Boy:
under the murmur of the women in the courtyard comes the
slow: low: barely audible pulsing of a plane swelling and
lapsing.*)

THE SICK WOMAN'S VOICE:
A day is longer . . . I was very young:
Everyone coming and looking and Isn't she young . . .

You sit in the dark and rest: you don't say anything . . .

THE ANNOUNCER:
Listen! Motor throbbing!

Probably one of their own.

No one watching it anyway.

THE SICK WOMAN'S VOICE:
The watercress between the crusts of water . . .

The wild iris in the water meadows:
The roses like the closing of desire . . .

And rest: you don't say anything . . .

THE ANNOUNCER:
There he is: we've got him!
One of the home ships.
He's combing the hills in circles:
Working heavily . . .
                    laboring . . .
Leveling now. He's high enough —
Spark in the sky when he hangs and the
Sun angles the fuselage:
Gone when the sunlight loses him:

Sound coming down out of nowhere:
Eddying: floating down.

No one noticing anyway:
No one looking or listening:
Only that sleepers waken . . .

A YOUNG MAN'S VOICE: (*close: low*)
  O are you there? Are you still there?
  I dreamed you had gone. Never go!

A GIRL'S VOICE: (*close: low*)
  Say we're happy. Tell me that we're happy.

THE YOUNG MAN'S VOICE:
  Stay as you are: do not move:
  Do not ever move: stay there:
  Stay with this sunlight on your shoulders . . .

THE ANNOUNCER:
  Still circling and wheeling.
  He's working the air as a hawk would —
  Stalking with height for cover:
  Hovering lost in sight.

  We see him and lose him and see him . . .

THE GIRL'S VOICE:
  Tell me we're happy. No but say we are.
  How can I know we are unless you tell me?
  How can a woman know the world is good?
  Which is the world and which is her and which is
  Things she's known for sure that never happened?
  She can't tell. She can't and be a woman.
  Can a cupful of well-water tell you the taste of the well-water?

THE YOUNG MAN'S VOICE:
  Stay with this sunlight on your shoulders:
  Stay with this sunlight on your hair.

THE ANNOUNCER:
We've lost him this time.

(*Over the voices of the lovers and the faint lapsing drone of the plane comes the Singing Woman's voice in a high clear scale: rising: descending.*)

Wait!
Wait! We've got him! He's doubled!
He's doubling back into sun:
He's running her east for the border . . .
Orders from somewhere certainly!

They've heard something or guessed it . . .

He was west of the town when he banked:
He yanked her round on a wing
Like swinging a colt on a bridle:
He's east of us now in the hills.

They've found something . . . or feared it!

(*A siren sounds at a distance like a hoarse parody of the Singing Woman's voice: rising, shrieking, descending. It is repeated under the voices, nearer and louder.*)

They've found it!

Feared and found!

There's the siren: the signal:
They've picked them up at the border . . .

THE BOY'S VOICE: (*shouting*)
Harry! Where are you Harry! Where are you! Where are you!

THE ANNOUNCER: (*dry and quick over the siren*)
Ten minutes to wait.

If they're cruising a hundred and eighty it's
Ten minutes: if less

111

More: if more less.
Ten we'd guess if we had to.
Depends how old they bring them.
The slow ones hobble the fast.

(*The siren rises to a crescendo.*)

Probably bringing the lot of them.
Strike at a king you must kill: —
You strike in sleep at a king
When you strike by trick at a people.
The treacherous wars must be quick
Or the victims live for the victory.

(*The siren dies rapidly away: the voices of the women have
been rising under it.*)

WOMEN'S VOICES:
Thank God that's over.

                Fit to deafen a woman.

Fit to deafen the cattle for twenty miles
And what for? For a war! To say there's another.

What's a war to us — there's always another.

All that noise to tell us there's a war.

Schoolboys banging the bells and blowing the bugles.

THE ANNOUNCER: (*women's voices under*)
Eight minutes more.

Town quiet: waiting:
Women's skirts in the court:
Women's arms in the windows:
Women's talk on the stair . . .

They lean there careless and talking:
Their shawls are bright in the doors:

The morning air's in their aprons:
They shape their hair with their hands:
They stand there softly and simply.

The women lean from the stairs.

WOMEN'S VOICES:
They're always waking us up for a war somewhere.
Get up! they say. We're at war!

                               It's no news!
Thousands of years they've been saying it.

                                    Crazy government!
Can't they run the country decent and quiet till
Eight in the morning even? The rest of the day
They can rule as loud as they like and as long as they mind to.
They can do what they want with the country from eight on.
Only till eight if they'd wait for the difficult sleepers —
Those that count their heartbeats every hour.

(*A police whistle blows at a distance: there are distant excited men's voices.*)

A WOMAN'S VOICE:
A woman's got no time to watch the wars —
Scrubbing the kitchens Tuesdays: marrying Mondays:
Bearing and burying — men to be born and to bury:
People dying never died before . . .

(*The whistle is nearer. The shouting men's voices become intelligible — some far: some nearer.*)

MEN'S VOICES:
Air Raid!

        Air Raid!

             Air Raid!

                Air Raid!

The bombers!

      The bombers!

            The bombers!

                  The bombers!

THE ANNOUNCER:
A police sergeant: he's shouting:
He's marching down through the street:
He's beating the shutters and shouting:
He's calling them out — "the cellars!"
Listen — "Take to the cellars!"
"Take to the church cellars!"
They only laugh: they lean from the
Open windows and laugh at him.

WOMEN'S VOICES:
You take the cellars!

      You can take them Sergeant!

Let the town policemen take the cellars!

They'll smell the mice in the cellars!

      Maybe they'll catch them!

(*The police whistle blows sharply.*)

THE VOICE OF THE SERGEANT: (*pompous: shouting*)
The alarm has been given. Five minutes have passed.
In five minutes more they must be here.
They are coming in numbers: I do not know how many.
The instructions are to occupy the vaults.
These are the orders of persons of proper authority.
You will march to the church by twos and at suitable intervals.

THE WOMEN'S VOICES:
Will we? And who'll be watching the pot while we're squat-
    ting there
Counting the mother spiders? The police?

There are frogs in the vaults.

                        There are also people's relations —
Not the kind that care to gossip either.

And who will iron the underwear now that it's sprinkled?

Oh the police will . . .

AN OLD WOMAN'S VOICE:
                        Listen to me policeman!
Perhaps it's true they're coming in their planes:
Perhaps it isn't true. But if it is
It's not for housewives in this town they're coming.
They're after the generals: they're after the cabinet ministers.
They're coming to capture the square in the capital city.
They always have: they always capture the city.
A fine sight we'd be — a parcel of housewives
Spinning with the spiders in a hole
While soldiers that don't know the hole is there
Or we are there or anything is there
Go running through the wonderful great sky
Hunting before and after for that city!

THE ANNOUNCER:
Six minutes gone.
Four more as we figure it.
If they picked them up to the right
We'll sight them over the river:
Horizon flat to the flight:
Rising or seeming to rise
As geese do coming inland.

Blur of light on the fins . . .

THE OLD WOMAN'S VOICE:
We're women. No one's making war on women —
The nation with no land: without history:
The nation whose dates are Sunday and Monday: the nation
Bounded by bread and sleep — by giving birth:
By taking death to keep: the ancient nation
Settled in the seasons of this earth as
Leaves are and oblivious as leaves:
Neutral as summer in the fierce divisions . . .

WOMEN'S VOICES:
They're always marching past to capture something!

It's all one if they march or they fly: they won't hurt us!

It's all one to us if they wing or they walk!

They've never troubled us yet!

They've never harmed us!

THE OLD WOMAN'S VOICE:
They never will. You are a new policeman.
Less than ten years you have been in this district.
I do not mention this to shame you: only
You do not know the history of this neighborhood.
We have seen such people in this place before.
They come in uniforms carrying elegant banners.
They march up and down. They ruin roads.
They interfere with the cattle. They rob the fruit trees.
They frighten calving cows. They trample clover.
No one would say they were likable people for visitors —
Making history over the corn and the cabbage:
Writing glorious pages in the beans:
Disturbing serious men in haying season.

116

Nevertheless it is true that few have suffered —
Maybe a girl would be rumpled a little . . .

(*There is a guffaw of women's laughter.*)

                                                    not many.

THE VOICE OF THE SERGEANT:
I do not say the order was expedient.
I say it was issued. I do not account for orders.
It is not my duty to account for orders.
Nevertheless it was issued by men of experience:
Persons of sound sense. It may have been thought
The wars have changed with the world and not for the better!

(*There is a burst of jeering laughter, the voice of the Sergeant
rising above it.*)

It may have been thought: this enemy kills women!

(*The laughter increases.*)

It may have been thought: this enemy kills women
Meaning to kill them!

(*The laughter rises to a shriek.*)

                    I say it may be thought
He makes his wars on women!

(*The laughter drops sharply away.*)

                              It may be thought
This enemy is not the usual enemy!
That this one is no general in a greatcoat
Conquering countries for the pride and praise:
That this one conquers other things than countries!

(*There is dead silence.*)

It may be thought that this one conquers life!

That life that won't be conquered can be killed!

That women are most lifelike! That he kills them!

It may be as I say. It may be thought he
Makes his wars on women . . . It is possible.

(*The women's voices rise again in a great shriek of laughter.
Over the laughter, clear and lifting and lovely as laughter itself
rises the Singing Woman's scale. Under it, dull, heavy, flat
come soft explosions.*)

WOMEN'S VOICES:
It's an ogre is coming!

> The devil is after us!

Hide in the church from the devil!

> I know him —
I've seen his face in the photographs. Oh but he's fierce!

THE ANNOUNCER: (*low and close*)
Listen . . .

A WOMAN'S VOICE:
He gets his photograph taken and sent around!

THE ANNOUNCER:
> Anti-aircraft!

A WOMAN'S VOICE:
He gets his photograph made in his belt and his buttons!

THE ANNOUNCER:
We can't see it: we hear it.

A WOMAN'S VOICE:
He gets his photograph made at the big parades!

THE ANNOUNCER:
Wait. There's a burst. There's another.

A WOMAN'S VOICE:
He gets his photograph made with his fist stuck out!

THE ANNOUNCER:
The first was the farther: they're nearing.

A WOMAN'S VOICE:
And his chin stuck out!

THE ANNOUNCER:
Another: nearer: another.

A WOMAN'S VOICE:
                              And his chest stuck out!

THE ANNOUNCER:
They follow each other like footsteps.
The steel stamps on the sky: the
Heel hits . . .
                    They hang like
Quills driven in sky: —
The quarry invisible . . .

(*An explosion is clearly heard.*)

                    Nearer . . .

(*The police whistle blows sharply. Under the voices the explosions are always louder. Under the explosions the inaudible
vibration of many planes swells painfully into heavy suffo-
cating sound.*)

THE VOICE OF THE SERGEANT:
You can hear for yourselves! You will now follow the orders —
To occupy the vaults of village churches:
In any event to descend from upper floors and
Scatter in streets avoiding visible gatherings . . .

WOMEN'S VOICES:
They're coming.

I hear them.

They're nearer.

A GIRL'S VOICE: (*frightened*)

They're nearer!

A WOMAN'S VOICE:

Ah they'll go over. There's nothing to fear: they'll go over.
They always do: they go over. Don't you fear.
Don't you fret. Don't you peer in the air — they'll
Go. They will. You'll forget they were ever by Saturday.

THE OLD WOMAN'S VOICE:

Dukes: Kings: Emperors — now there's this kind.
They're all fools — the lot of them: always were:
Marching around with their drums: shooting their guns off!
Let them step till they stop if it gives them pleasure.
It's all one to us if they do or they don't.
We needn't crick our necks to watch it . . .

(*The roar of the planes increases in slow oppressive crescendo.
The explosions are no longer heard.*)

THE ANNOUNCER:

We hear them: we can't see them.

We hear the shearing metal:
We hear the tearing air.

All we see is sun.

Sun: the hawk's ambush.

Their flight is from the sun.
They might be low: they might be
Well down — three thousand.
They might be less.

They are many:
Hard to guess how many . . .

(*rapidly*)

We've got them now: we see them:
They're out of the dazzle: they're flying
Fighting formation in column
Squadron following squadron
Ten — fifteen squadrons
Bombing models mostly
Big ones: three motors . . .

Not so low as we figured them . . .

Almost over . . .

(*The roar of the planes breaks: rises sharply in pitch: diminishes: the women's voices above it.*)

WOMEN'S VOICES:
Look!

Look! Look! Look!

THE ANNOUNCER: (*rapidly*)
They're changing formation they're banking
The whole flight is banking
Front wheeling to flank
Flank anchored and climbing
Climbing bank into line . . .

The line swung like a lariat!

WOMEN'S VOICES:
Look! It's circling as a bird does!

It circles as a hawk would circle hunting!

It's hunting us under the roof: the room: the curtain!

THE ANNOUNCER:
   They're wheeling round for the town
   They're rounding in by the river
   They're giving it throttle they're climbing
   The timing is perfect they're flying with
   Perfect precision of timing
   Perfect mechanical certainty . . .

WOMEN'S VOICES:
   Show it our skirts!

                        Show it our shawls!

   All of us: into the street all of us!

THE ANNOUNCER:
   They turn like stones on a string:
   They swing like steel in a groove:
   They move like tools not men:
   You'd say there were no men:
   You'd say they had no will but the
   Will of motor on metal . . .

   (*The roar of the planes increases from moment to moment.*)

WOMEN'S VOICES:
   Show it our skirts in the street: it won't hurt us!

   Show it our softness! Show it our weakness!

   Show it our womanhood!

                        Into the street!

   Into the street all of us!

                        All of us!

   (*The pitch of the roar opens: the sound is huge, brutal, close.*)

THE ANNOUNCER:
   They swing: the wing dips:

There's the signal: the dip: they'll
Dive: they're ready to dive:
They're steady: they're heading down:
They're dead on the town: they're nosing:
They're easing over: they're over:
There they go: there they —

(*A crazy stammering of machine guns hammers above the rising roar.*)

A WOMAN'S VOICE: (*shrieking*)
It's us do you see!

A WOMAN'S VOICE: (*shrieking*)
       It's us don't you see us!

(*For an instant the shrieking voices of the women, the shattering noise of the guns and the huge scream of the planes are mingled, then the voices are gone and the guns are gone and the scream of the planes closes to a deep sustained music note level and long as silence. After a moment comes the Boy's voice rising on each word, breaking off.*)

THE BOY'S VOICE:
Harry!   Harry!   Harry! . . .

(*The diminishing music note again —level — long.*)

THE VOICE OF THE YOUNG MAN:

Stay as you are: do not move:
Do not ever move . . .

(*The diminishing music note again. Over it the voice of the Singing Woman rising in a slow screaming scale of the purest agony broken at last on the unbearably highest note. The diminishing drone of the planes fades into actual silence.*)

THE END

123

The Trojan Horse

Preface

When *The Trojan Horse* was published in 1952, Houghton Mifflin circulated a "limited edition, not for sale" with a publisher's note by Paul Brooks which ended with this sentence: "If this play helps us to recognize a wooden horse when we see one it will have served an important purpose."

What Paul Brooks had in mind, of course, was the incredible reception given in that year by a great part of the American people to Senator Joe McCarthy's publicity campaign against the great Republic. In 1952, and for several years before, the United States had stood at the towering height of its greatest triumph. It had played the central role in the winning of the Second World War, the most remarkable of all military victories. It had destroyed Hitler and Hitlerism in the two hemispheres of the earth. It was recognized as the most powerful nation in the modern world. It believed in itself. It believed in its institutions, its form of government, the human freedom for which it had fought. And yet, when an insignificant and unrespected member of the United States Senate launched an attack on the integrity of the American government he was supported by so large a body of American opinion that even his bravest and most admired opponents in the Senate were silenced for a time.

The Department of State, McCarthy told the listening world, was crowded with card-carrying Communists. There was no proof, no pretence at proof, but McCarthy said it and millions apparently believed him. There were traitors, he said, everywhere in the government of the Republic, even in the Department of War. Again there was no proof: there never had been proof and never would be but he had said it and he was believed. Even the people themselves, he said, were guilty of treason: teachers, students, librarians, intellectuals, scientists, actors and actresses, artists, writers — above all actors and actresses and writers. The country was rotten with Communism. There were spies and conspirators under every bed.

The whole thing, seen now in retrospect, was a patent fraud — a fraud as obvious as the Trojan Horse itself with those armed Greeks hidden in its belly. But even so, there was a mystery in one as in the other. Why had the Trojans taken the huge horse in, breaching their own walls to let it pass? Why had our deluded generation of Americans accepted McCarthy's enormous fabrication made, not of wood but lies, and set it up in the hearing rooms of the Senate to threaten not the Communists but the country?

Our minds — those of us who thought of these things, and we all did — went back to Homer who must have known. "A poet, a man who knows the world" says Homer through the mouth of the king of the Phaeacians in Robert Fitzgerald's new translation of the *Odyssey*. What did Homer know that we did not know of that enormous horse the Greeks left on the shore when they sailed off for home — pretended to sail off? We read the story over and over wondering.

Here is one reading of it.

A. MacL.

PRELUDE

Mewing of gulls, slow beat of the sea. A girl's voice and an old man's. They seem to stand beside us as they speak.

THE GIRL:
Old poet, old blind wandering man,
Tell me why the town goes down,
Tell me by what hand it falls . . .

(The shrieking of the gulls overwhelms her voice at the word "falls" and drowns the Old Man's answer.)

THE GIRL:
I cannot hear you for the sea gulls.
Why does that great city fall?

OLD MAN:
The wooden horse and the Swan's daughter . . .

THE GIRL:
I cannot hear you!

OLD MAN:
                    The Swan's daughter.
They brought the horse within the walls.
Some said the Greeks were in it. She
touched it three times with her hands.

129

THE GIRL:
Who touched it?

OLD MAN:
                    Helen. Named their names.
  I think they answered for she ran.
  Greek though she was she feared the Greeks so.

THE GIRL:
Helen! What walls are these? What city?

OLD MAN:
Troy and her people on that shore.

(*The sea, the gulls, a chatter of excited voices off beyond. A child's voice screaming above the others.*)

                                *

CHILD:
A horse! Look at the horse!
A wood horse!

WOMAN:
                    Don't
Touch it! Don't go near it!

CHILD:
Look at its eyes staring!
Look at its eyes! It has white
Eyes!

WOMAN:
            Keep back I tell you!

YOUNG WOMAN:
I don't see a horse.

MAN:
You would if that cow moved over.

WOMAN:
Who are you calling cow?

MAN:
Forgive it, Lady. I see
Badly at sun-up.

WOMAN:
You'll see
Worse with your eyes scratched out!
Forgive it, he says!

CHILD:
Horses are
Trojan aren't they? You told me
Horse is for Troy. Is *that* horse?
Is that horse Trojan? Is it?

MAN:
Call that a horse!
That thing is a monument!
Ten natural horses
Sixteen hands at the withers
Wouldn't outweigh it, the lot of them.

BLIND MAN:
Lead me a little nearer.
Have the Councillors come?

GIRL:
Not yet.

BLIND MAN:
They started at dawn didn't they?
You told me how they started:
Each, you said, with his neck out
Hissing at the dogs like
Geese — a file of geese!

131

Girls should respect the old,
Particularly Councillors:
Who will respect them if girls don't?

GIRL:

I think those Councillors would have been here
Long since but for the green things.
After all these years cooped up
When everything outside the wall,
Even the dock plants and the mullen,
Grew the other side of danger —
After all that time to touch
The dock plants and the dusty mullen
Made even their hearts jump. I think
They stood there gawking at the green things.

BLIND MAN:

What are they saying of the god,
Those shouting women?

GIRL:

That the horse is
God's.

WOMAN: (*shouting*)
Only a god could have made it!

WOMAN: (*shouting*)
It's God's work!

WOMAN: (*shouting*)
The Greeks knew that.
They launched ship when they saw it —
Took to the sea.

BOY:

They did, too.
I was the one that found it.

Hearing the Greeks had gone
I crossed fields to the foreshore.
The whole beach was burning —
Bone-stink, stench of straw.
Looming in dirty dawn
I looked left and I saw it!
Oh, they fled I tell you:
I did! *I* ran!

OLD WOMAN:

                    Aye!
That's what they left us — stench
Of ten years' war on the wind,
Ten years' trash on the beaches:
Grooves of their keels in our gravel;
Graves of our sons in the sand . . .

BOY:

Oh, I ran! I ran!
I liked to have choked in that smother.
Every broken thing,
Old chariots, arrows,
Shirts, ropes, shoes,
Iron pots, fish-heads,
Dead men in their barrows,
Stench from the burnt latrines,
The whole beach one bonfire!

OLD WOMAN:

Terror had taken them! Ah,
Terror had taken them!

MAN:

                    Big!
Why should it not be big?
What this city needs

Is one overmastering monument
Bringing the god-head in!
Town that gets in a war
For a girl's looks, fights
Ten mortal years
Not on the husband's side —
The bed and the bed's duty;
Piety, order, restraint —
No! On the lover's side!
It's your choice, we told him,
And the girl — the girl's beautiful:
Swan's daughter and beautiful!
So we fought for their right to be happy!
Curious thing to be killed for:
The right to choose and be happy!

MAN:

Can you think of a better?

MAN:

                                    Peace! —
Peace! Order! Certainty!
Things in their proper places!
Respect for authority! Truth!
A war like that can be won, —
The town gates open,
Grass to walk on, quietness.
The god will fight in such battles:
Not in our kind. Happiness!

WOMAN:

Things as they were in the old time!
The young girls in the meadows,
Mushrooms, the nights for sleep.

MAN:

Oh the Greeks will be back.
The Greeks will be back. You'll see them.
The Greeks believe in the oracles.

MAN:

Mount that horse in Troy
And we too will have oracles —
Better than oracles — god-help!

MAN:

We help ourselves in this city.

MAN:

And what has it gotten us? War!

MAN:

We're still here, aren't we?
After the ten long years
And the toll of men and of horses
And all that talk we're here!
We're still here! The town too.

WOMAN:

Toll, he says! The toll!
Days that you buy with dead men!
Nights that you buy with fear!

MAN:

How else would you buy them?

WOMAN:

                              Trust

God!

WOMAN:

Drag the horse in!

WOMAN:
  Only the god can defend us!

GIRL:
  They're coming.

BLIND MAN:
                Who?

GIRL:
                The Councillors.

BLIND MAN:
  Each with his mind made up and hung
  Like dinner on a stick's end in a napkin?

MAN: (*shouting*)
  Order! The Council in order!

WOMAN:
  The wise men are ready.

WOMAN:
                Ready as
  Wise men ever are.

WOMAN:
  Would you know? I thought the wise ones
  Left you alone.

MAN: (*shouting*)
                Order!

MAN:
  Know what she said when she saw it?

MAN:
  Saw what?

MAN:
              The horse.

136

MAN:

 Who?

MAN:

   I told you: Cassandra.
 The prophetic girl, Cassandra.

MAN:

 You shouldn't talk to Cassandra.
 What did she say? She's mad.

MAN:

 Cassandra said when she saw it:
 "Who rides the horse that has no rider?"
 Those were her actual words.

MAN:

 Poor girl! They should watch her.

MAN:

 How can they watch what she hears?
 She hears voices speaking:
 At least she thinks she hears them.

GIRL:

 They're around the enormous horse now,
 Each with his spear of rank:
 Even the old one, Laocoön.

BLIND MAN:

 With his sons to hold his arms up?

GIRL:

 Why should a man so old
 Carry the spear?

BLIND MAN:

   For dignity.

137

FIRST COUNCILLOR:
  Councillors!

GIRL:
                    That's the king's man speaking.

FIRST COUNCILLOR:
  Give me your judgments what we have to do.
  The Greeks have drawn their ships off, gone to sea,
  Burnt their encampments, vanished. This remains.
  No one believes the ten year war is ended.
  Those Greeks have a terrible certainty. They think
  The eternal future of the world is spun
  In one thread and the thread is theirs. They think
  The fall of Troy has been foredoomed and uttered.
  And yet they draw their keels off and this stands here:
  Horse, Troy's emblem, guardian of the city,
  Perfect in every part of life but one —
  The natural scale has been exceeded; horse but
  Monstrous! Whether god or Greek has done this;
  Whether the Greeks have made it or have fled from it;
  Whether we should haul the thing to Troy
  Or let it rot here, answer each in turn.
  You first.

SECOND COUNCILLOR:
                    Receive it. That the Greeks have fled
  This wind is proof enough. That hot stale stench
  Is terror's, tumbled headlong into ships,
  The proud tents fired with precipitate hands
  Too frightened to sort out the useful wool
  Or save the bed sacks but the lot left smoldering.
  I know that smell of dread. All captains know it.
  What the Greeks fear must be friend to Troy.

SHOUTING VOICE:
 Horse will defend us!

SHOUTING VOICE:
                Drag the horse in!

FIRST COUNCILLOR:
                         You.

THIRD COUNCILLOR:
 I say what he says: that the Greeks have fled.
 I do not say the Greeks are gone. No sensible
 Ripe experienced man would make that judgment.
 These Greeks will still return and still return
 And still again return until the prophecy,
 Scored, they think, upon the skull of time,
 Has been accomplished and this town, its towers
 Tumbled upon our heap of bones, becomes
 Our sepulchre, not our city. We shall need
 Friends to survive this struggle — powerful friends —
 The greatest and most powerful — Him the thunder
 Runs from, muttering down the hollow sky,
 And seas have fled from, that on ultimate shoals
 Shatter themselves and perish. If this shape,
 Made in the noble image of a horse,
 Is His or comes from Him and we befriend it
 God will befriend *us*. The proud painted horse
 Will bring the god in on our side to fight for us.

MAN: (*shouting*)
 Bring the god in!

MAN: (*shouting*)
                Bring the horse in and the god
 Fights for us Trojans!

139

MAN: (*shouting*)
>God is in it!

FIRST COUNCILLOR:
>   You,
>Laocoön.

LAOCOÖN:
>   You think the god is in it?
>You think the god needs that great coopered tun,
>Those towering knees to trot him into Troy?
>You think there are not others than the god
>Might need them more than He does — that Light Foot
>That comes to each man's wonder, but alone?
>Are you so sure this swollen shape is Trojan?
>Perhaps I have forgotten. I am old.
>I thought Troy's horse was carved upon a coin,
>An image on a ring, that each man fingered
>Privately and as his heart was moved.
>No Trojan would have made Troy's horse a monument,
>Enormous as a public tomb, where multitudes
>Mincing beneath it on a marble stair
>Must stand or squat or knuckle all together.
>Troy was not worshiped: Troy was loved. And now
>You stand here by this monumental image
>Shaped like Troy's horse and say the god is in it —
>Heaven's authority and man's in one!
>You think its stature is the proof of God:
>The greater the more sacred. Is it?

THIRD COUNCILLOR:
>   Gods and
>Men bear witness what he says is true.
>Troy's horse was each man's signet on his finger,
>Boss to his thumb. Should we be proud for that?

The Greeks have penned us ten years in this city,
Each with his private emblem in his palm, —
Each with his clay horse or his gold or silver.
Terrified of that ambush in the dark,
Those skulking secret lurkers, each man touched
The meaning hidden in his hand to help him.
What Troy has lacked these years is one great monument,
Common to all of us, to top the town
And stand there staring with its god's conviction,
Sleepless, keeping pure the holy air
As great trees keep the air pure.

FIRST COUNCILLOR:

                                   You, Laocoön, — .
You have not given judgment what to do.

LAOCOÖN:

There is a cliff just here. Let it be toppled
Headlong from that cliff into the sea,
The horse and all it holds.

SHOUTING VOICES:

                              No!
                                   No!

The horse is Trojan!
                         Treason!
                                   The god is in it!

Blasphemy!

THIRD COUNCILLOR:

               Be patient, Trojans. This old man,
Venerated over years as soldier,
Councillor, ministrant at public altars —
This reverend, long-honored, gray old man,
Speaks what he has not well considered.

141

SHOUTING VOICES:

Blasphemy!

The god is in it!

Bring the god in!

Treason!

Treason! . . .

(*The voices break off: there is a sudden silence.*)

BLIND MAN:

Why are they suddenly so still —
Like frogs that hear the heron in the lilies?

GIRL:

Laocoön has risen, his long spear
Balanced upon his hand.

BLIND MAN:

He threatens them?

GIRL:

The horse, not them.

LAOCOÖN:

You need not fear me, Trojans.
I am not armed to harm you but to heal.
There is a hidden word that you must hear
If Troy is not to perish. Not my word! —
Your ears are deaf to me now — but a word
Even the deafness in your hearts will hear.
Listen, you Trojans! . . .

(*A gasp is heard; a breathless silence, then the heavy stroke of
the javelin on the hollow reverberating wood and a man's sudden muffled cry, as suddenly stilled. Then silence. Then . . .*)

WOMAN:

Something cried out . . .

WOMAN:
                    A voice cried . . .

MAN:
                                                Struck
    By dark and wakened into death
    A man would cry so . . .

LAOCOÖN:
                        And what man?
    Ten years you've heard those voices. What man?

WOMAN:
    I heard a cry and silenced . . .

MAN:
                                I heard
    A man's cry and cut off and silence . . .

BLIND MAN: (*voices under*)
    Where is Laocoön?

GIRL: (*voices under*)
                        He's gone
    His sons beside him at each shoulder.
    They climb the sea path toward the city.

BLIND MAN:
    His work is done. They know the truth now.
    They know what god is in that monument.

GIRL:
    Some keep watch around it. Some
    Lash the great hawsers to the hocks.
    None speak. They shake their heads and grin
    And mutter and stare sideways at it.

143

BLIND MAN:
  Angrier with themselves than it!
  A man some seeming gentle dog,
  Made much of and brought home, has bitten,
  Suffers more in pride than finger.
  Where are you leading me?

GIRL:
                              It's here
  The cliff breaks and they'll drown it . . . Here . . .
  How clear the water is — how clear!
  You cannot see it, not the water,
  Not the surface ripple of the water:
  Only the ropes of sun far under
  Knotting and unknotting on the sand
  That delicate slow web the waves weave.

BLIND MAN:
  You show it well.

  (*sound of the sea far down and of the gulls*)

GIRL:
                  I heard Cassandra
  Muttering something when the voice cried.

BLIND MAN:
  Oh Cassandra's always muttering.
  Nobody listens to her.

GIRL:
                  You did.

BLIND MAN:
  How far the sea sound is! Cassandra?
  Oh a kind of jingle.

GIRL:

Tell me.

BLIND MAN:

A child's song. You could bounce a ball to it.
"Whose hand is that upon the bridle?
Whose voice cries out, Destroy! Destroy!
Who rides the horse that has no rider?"
Something like that. I don't remember.

GIRL:

That's not a child's song.

BLIND MAN:

There is someone
Shouting . . . A great way off . . . The wind
Veers . . .

GIRL:

I hear him. Now I see him.
All of them see him. On the cliff there.

BLIND MAN:

Where the path goes up to Troy?
What is he shouting to us? Listen!

(*silence . . . the sea far down; the gulls mewing . . . the
distant shouting voice . . . the words caught in the flaws of
the wind and carried . . .*)

GIRL:

Something about Laocoön he's saying . . .
Sons also . . . serpents . . .

BLIND MAN:

Serpents!
What does he say of serpents?

145

GIRL:
                              The wind
Carries the words like leaves . . . He's dead!
Laocoön is dead! . . . His sons
Dead! . . . Serpents from the sea
Slavered with silver slime strangled them . . .

BLIND MAN:
Serpents he says. Slavered he says.
I see the slaver, not the serpents.
Who followed when Laocoön went?
He did. Now he finds him strangled.

GIRL:
. . . came from the sea far out . . . others they
Passed . . . him strangled . . . high on the
Stony strath they took him . . . afterward,
Silver, they returned to sea . . .

(*silence*)

The shouting man has gone.

WOMAN:
                              Others they
Passed . . .

WOMAN:
          Him only!

WOMAN:
               Silver!

FIRST COUNCILLOR:
It was the god that sent this, certainly.

BLIND MAN:
Who spoke then?

146

GIRL:
  The king's man: the Councillor.

FIRST COUNCILLOR:
  His sons too! Both his sons!

SECOND COUNCILLOR:
                          The god
  Punished him!

THIRD COUNCILLOR:
                    The god will punish
  All who question the great horse!

BLIND MAN:
  Councillors should speak for counsel.
  Why do they menace us with words?

THIRD COUNCILLOR:
  Now are you satisfied, you Trojans?
  Laocoön is satisfied.
  He has no questions anymore.

SECOND COUNCILLOR:
  He knows what voice it was, what sacred
  Voice that answered when the spear struck.
  Which of you does not know? Which one?

  (*silence*)

THIRD COUNCILLOR:
  Which of you heard a Greek cry?

  (*silence*)

                              None?

  (*silence*)

BLIND MAN:
Whatever they heard they did not hear it.
After that silence of Laocoön's
Nothing they thought they knew is known.

THIRD COUNCILLOR:
Oh there are Greek cries if you want them!
Wait till the ships come back! You'll hear
Not one alone, but thousands — thousands —
Screaming upon your walls, your roofs,
Before your doors, among your gardens.
Think of those cries to come! Oh think of
Them! And will the god defend you?
We know now what the horse is, all of us.
We are his witnesses: God's witnesses.
Will God defend us when the Greeks come?

GIRL: (*the ranting voice beneath her voice*)
What will they do?

BLIND MAN:
                    They cannot tell.
They are no longer sure of anything.
They thought the horse was holy. Then
The horse was questioned and that voice confessed.
Now the questioner is silenced.

GIRL:
Not the voice though. I can hear it
Choking in that terrible cry.
I think they all must hear it, all of them.
What will they do?

BLIND MAN:
                    Why, what they must do.
Drag the enormous thing to Troy.

148

GIRL:

How will they bring it through the gateway?
The gate is narrow.

BLIND MAN:

Through the wall then.

GIRL:

They say the builders made it narrow
Meaning only men should pass
And only one man and then one man.

WOMAN:

Why do you talk against the horse?
Those who talk against the horse
Talk against Troy, against religion.

GIRL:

I only said the gate was narrow.

WOMAN:

You spoke against it. If you speak so
I for one will not be near you.
I do not know your name. You might be
Anyone — Helen's woman even —
A Greek girl or a friend of Greeks.

GIRL:

I am of Troy! Look at me! Look at me!

WOMAN:

Talk to yourself. I do not know you.

BLIND MAN:

The horse has entered Troy.

GIRL:

Oh no . . .

It stands there waiting.

149

BLIND MAN:
                        Nevertheless
The horse has entered Troy. I heard it.

GIRL:
You mean that woman's voice who spoke to me?
Why did she speak so?

BLIND MAN:
                        Out of fear.
Bring that enormous image in
To make official patriots of us,
Sweating our public love by law,
And all of us will fear each other.

SHOUTING VOICE:
Break the blocks out!

VOICES: (*distant*)
                        Blocks out!

SHOUTING VOICE:
                              Ropes!

VOICES: (*distant*)
Make fast the ropes! . . . the ropes! . . .

SHOUTING VOICE:
                              Ready!

SHOUTING VOICE AND DISTANT VOICES: (*antiphonally*)
Now! . . . Heave! . . . Now! . . . Heave! . . .

GIRL: (*the voices under*)
Five hundred men there must be
Tugging and toiling at those ropes . . .
Ants around a great dead fly!

THE VOICES: (*under*)
  Ho! There she rolls . . .
        There she rolls . . .
          She's rolling . . .

WOMEN'S VOICES: (*over the shouting and rumbling*)
  Oh but it's huge!
    Lurching and leaning!
  Hear how it thunders!
    Ah, the huge horse!

(*the rumbling sound of the horse, the shouting*)

GIRL: (*over*)
  It stumbles over stones as stiff
  And clumsy as a new-born colt
  But monstrous too. No! There's something
  Terrible in that heavy moving!

BLIND MAN: (*over*)
  Listen!

GIRL:
        Why do you touch me so?

BLIND MAN:
  That sound!

GIRL:
          What sound?

BLIND MAN:
                  That sound beneath the
  Wood sound!

GIRL:
          What beneath the wood sound?
  I don't hear it. All I hear
  Is hollow wood on stony ground.

BLIND MAN:
Each time the timber rumbles,
Each time the planking pounds,
Something soft that falls and catches.

GIRL:
Something after when the wood sounds . . .

BLIND MAN:
Listen!

GIRL:
     Then!

(*The rumbling and shouting break off.*)

BLIND MAN:
     They've heard it!

GIRL:
Those beside the horse have heard it.
Now they all have. If the ropes were
Snakes they could not fling them farther.

SECOND COUNCILLOR:
Pull! You'll lose the horse!

MAN:
     There's something
Moves in that belly!

MAN:
     Something living
Moves in that belly when the horse moves.

MAN:
Something that's alive and listens.

MAN:
Rustles and listens.

THIRD COUNCILLOR:
                    Are you men
Or not men? Take the ropes up! Take them!

BLIND MAN:
Even if the death within there
Called its name out and its time,
That Councillor would not believe it.
What takes the shape of Troy is Trojan.
What talks of God is God's. He knows!

THIRD COUNCILLOR:
There was a man once named Laocoön.
Have you forgotten him? He learned
What some among you have not learned.
He asked and the god answered him.

MAN:
There was a cry that answered.

WOMAN:
                        What was that
Cry, that cry?

THIRD COUNCILLOR:
               The god destroyed him.

WOMAN:
What was that choking cry?

THIRD COUNCILLOR:
                     His sons too.

WOMAN:
What was that cry, that cry, that cry?

FIRST COUNCILLOR:
If the god can't persuade you, who can persuade you?

153

GIRL: (*whispering*)
Helen is standing in the field.

BLIND MAN:
Helen? Helen you say?

GIRL:
                                        Beside the
Olives.

BLIND MAN:
Lead me toward the Councillors.

(*stirring, movement, muttering voices of the crowd as they press through it*)

GIRL: (*whispering*)
They stand beyond you, not ten paces.
One of them turns his head now.

BLIND MAN:
                                        Councillors,
You say the god cannot persuade us.
Are you so sure? For there is one,
Though not, I think, a god that can: —
One that is not far off.

FIRST COUNCILLOR:
                                        What one?

BLIND MAN:
A woman.

SECOND COUNCILLOR:
                  What woman? What can she do?

BLIND MAN:
What all men know that she can do —
A woman who is most a woman:
Helen.

154

THIRD COUNCILLOR:
　　Helen!

BLIND MAN:
　　　　　　　I think she hears you.
They say she stands there by the olives.

THIRD COUNCILLOR:
　　Oh Helen's beautiful, no question:
　　The one wholly beautiful woman,
　　Not one finger bone averse
　　Or foot bone or least fault of carriage.
　　We have no quarrel with her beauty:
　　A woman such as all men think
　　Some woman must be and they'll find her.
　　Helen is beautiful enough,
　　But what can Helen know of such things?

SECOND COUNCILLOR:
　　What can Helen know of Troy
　　Or Troy's great holy image?

BLIND MAN:
　　　　　　　　　　Some,
　　Deceived no doubt by their own senses,
　　Think Troy's image may conceal
　　Troy's enemies.

FIRST COUNCILLOR:
　　　　　　　And how can she,
Beautiful though she is, persuade them?

BLIND MAN:
　　Because she is! Women hear heartbeats
　　Even behind the holiest appearances.
　　Treason betrays itself with women,

155

And most with those most beautiful. No woman
Ever was beautiful as Helen is:
Ten years the Greeks have fought to take her,
Thought of her thighs, her walk, her voice —
Mostly her voice, for each one carries it
Sweet as a raisin in remembrance.
If Helen whispered they would answer her.
Even if she barely touched
The shell that hid them they would answer:
If there are hidden Greeks they'll answer.

THIRD COUNCILLOR:
And if none answer?

BLIND MAN:
                    There is no one.

MAN:
Let Helen call the Greeks!

MAN:
                          Let Helen
Speak to them!

MAN:
                    Bring Helen near them!

WOMAN:
Yes, bring Helen! If those Greeks
Are like the men of this town, bring her!
There's not a man of you in Troy
But Helen, if she whistled for him,
Even if he squatted to his need,
Or Ajax chased him, or he lay
In bed at love, would leap and sing out
Here! I'm here!

156

WOMAN:
                    Let Helen call!
It's she they sleep with, every man of them.
Whatever the poor creature in their arms
It's she they hold there. Let her call!
She's tall and golden!

WOMAN:
                                And our hair
Is not gold always and our hands
Withered with water and the work
To keep a house fit and a man fed
Three times in the blessed day,
Sluicing the gutters out at night.

WOMAN:
All we know is men, not horses.

WOMAN:
It's enough, too!

MAN:
                    Quiet, can't you?
Helen will hear you caw.

WOMAN:
                            She won't though.
Beauty is a kind of deafness.
Beautiful women have that look
Of listening that Helen has
As though she heard a music inward.
No tune that we could play would touch her.

FIRST COUNCILLOR:
Turn your head. She stands beside you.

HELEN:
I think you speak my name . . .

157

BLIND MAN:
  It has been spoken.

FIRST COUNCILLOR:
                    Some, contentious,
  Argue that the horse of Troy,
  Grown greater than a horse, hides Greeks.
  The god has silenced one such. Still they
  Talk. They say if Helen touched it,
  Greeks, if there were Greeks, would answer her.

WOMAN:
  Perhaps your husband, Menelaus,
  If he lies hidden there will answer!

MAN:
  Shame! For shame!

FIRST COUNCILLOR:
                    Be quiet, both of you.

HELEN:
  Why should Menelaus answer?
  You think he comes for me? To take me?
  That was a long time back. He comes
  To put away now, not to take . . .
  To put the past away, not take it.

WOMAN:
  You think they would not take you, Lady?
  After ten years of war you think
  The prize of war would not be taken?

HELEN:
  Taken? . . .
                    Yes, I should be taken.
  Not as before though — not as then
  In haste and darkness and desire

Borne from the bedside down to ship,
And by the ship from shore, the oar-beat
Thudding in the thole pins like a heart,
Thick and thicker till the headland
Opened and the wind came, the ship shuddered
Rising the first sea-surge, and suddenly
Silence and the singing keel,
The sail set . . .

(*silence*)

              Taken! Not as then though,
Feeling the sail fill and the silver peak
swing through the channels of the stars . . .

(*silence*)

Why should Menelaus answer me?
He comes to put the past away:
To cancel out this town, this hope, this
Troy that in contempt of fate
Chose one man's happiness to fight for —
And one woman's — and made fate contemptible
And all who serve their fate. He comes
To scratch that sweetness out of time
And overwrite it with the certainties
Soldiers, when the towns are taken,
Scrawl in ordure on dead walls . . .

What must I do?

MAN:
              Why, call their names:
Speak to them, Lady.

MAN:
              But go near it.
Touch the belly with your hands.

159

HELEN:
I do not wish to touch it.

FIRST COUNCILLOR:
                           Those
Who love Troy touch the things of Troy.

HELEN:
I have more reason to love Troy
Than any Trojan . . . except one . . .
Who had my reason. But this monstrous,
Staring, swollen image . . .

MAN:
                              Only
Touch it! Name them!

MAN:
                    Name their names!

WOMAN:
Yes, name them, Lady! You can name them! —
Diomedes. Menelaus.

WOMAN:
You know that Menelaus, Helen!

FIRST COUNCILLOR:
Do not mind these others, Lady.
Speak the names once: Menelaus,
Diomedes, him of Ithaca.
Speak where those within could hear —
If there were men within.

HELEN:
                         But why should
Enemies of Troy take hiding
There in the shape of Troy?

MAN:

For hiding!

FIRST COUNCILLOR:
Speak to them.

GIRL:

She's touched it!

BLIND MAN:

Listen!

GIRL:
They said her arms were beautiful. I think
Nothing is beautiful as her arms.

BLIND MAN:
What does she say?

GIRL:

I cannot hear . . .
One word: "Diomedes."

BLIND MAN:

Murderer!
Bloody-knuckled, brutal murderer!

HELEN: (*whispering*)
Odysseus!

GIRL:

Odysseus.

BLIND MAN:
I hear her. Listen!

HELEN: (*whispering*)

Menelaus!

(*silence*)

MAN:

There is no answer. Nothing.

HELEN:

Nothing!

SECOND COUNCILLOR:

What could answer her but nothing?
What did you hope for? — that the pine would
Utter? That the wooden horse would
Speak? Or do you think the god
Converses with all questioners?

MAN:

Say
Something, Lady, that will name you:
Something they will know your name by —
Those who lie there — if they lie there.

FIRST COUNCILLOR:

Why do you plague her? She has answered you.

HELEN:

I have no words to say . . .

Odysseus! . . .
Odysseus, are you so long
In silence of a woman's voice
You cannot hear me calling to you?

(*silence*)

Or is it your ear, Menelaus,
Words of mine are dumb to? For they say
Those who have loved and have forgotten
Cannot encounter. The returning ghost,
Cry though it may against the door
Or in the chamber even, meets
Unknowing the returning ghost.

THIRD COUNCILLOR:
    You have your ears: I mine: and I hear
    Nothing!

FIRST COUNCILLOR:
            No one has answered her.

HELEN:
    He does not speak. He would have heard me
    Close as my lips are now. One night
    The southwest winter wind piled up
    Tumultuous surges on that beach
    Until the whole house trembled. The sea sound
    Could not awaken him but one
    Quick whispered word awakened him.
    He woke . . .

BLIND MAN:
            What is it?

GIRL:
                    Oh she stares!
    She stands there with her motionless hands
    Hard on her breasts and stares at us!

BLIND MAN:
                    She hears it.

FIRST COUNCILLOR:
    Speak to us, Lady. Do not stand there
    Staring at us with those eyes
    That see, not us but see!

GIRL:
                A hare,
    Frozen in her form, that feels
    The gray hawk circle, would be still
    As she is!

THIRD COUNCILLOR:
     If you do not speak
Some fool will say he answered you —
That Menelaus answered.

HELEN:
                              No!
Not answered . . .
                    No! Oh no! Oh no!

GIRL:
    She's gone. She's running through the trees.
    Why does she run so?

    (*a distant throbbing sound; a slow, dull pulse*)

BLIND MAN:
                         Oh, she knows.
    She has no people anymore.
    If she should tell the truth these Trojans
    Mad in their terror would destroy her.
    If she is silent, then those others —
    Those that have hunted her so long —
    Will take her in the night. She runs.

    (*The throbbing sound is louder.*)

GIRL:
    What sound is that as though a heartbeat?

BLIND MAN:
    The ram against the walls of Troy.
    The wall must break to take the horse in.

GIRL:
    Is that the ram sound now, that pounding?
    Why are they shouting in the town?

BLIND MAN:
Perhaps the wall has fallen . . . as a wave breaks
Crumbling at its curling crest,
Flinging its whole weight forward, falling.

(*The throbbing sound changes to music.*)

GIRL:
And music! And that music!

BLIND MAN:
The enormous
Horse has entered Troy. The god
Defends us from our enemies!

GIRL:
Oh stop them! Stop them! . . .

BLIND MAN:
Nothing I or anyone can do,
Nothing can change it now. They shout
And their own shouting deafens them.

(*The sound of the distant music rises: there is a woman's sobbing.*)

Who stands there weeping by the water?

GIRL:
Cassandra.

BLIND MAN:
Why do you weep Cassandra?

CASSANDRA:
My city is burning.

BLIND MAN:
No, not burning.

CASSANDRA:
I hear them shrieking in their beds.

GIRL:
They are bringing the Trojan horse in, Cassandra.
That's what you hear — the shouting.

CASSANDRA:
                                        The smoke smell
Chokes me.

GIRL:
                It is dust where the wall is broken:
Only the dust, Cassandra.

CASSANDRA:
                        It chokes me —
The smoke smell chokes me . . .

                                And the smell of blood.

(*a distant triumphant shout: a blare of trumpets*)

(*in a childish sing-song*)

What hand is that upon the bridle?
What voice cries out Destroy! Destroy!
Who rides the horse that has no rider?
No other hand shall burn Troy!

THE END

166

This Music Crept by Me upon the Waters

Preface

There is a phrase of Iris Origo's which could serve as epigraph to this play: "the visionary world of Far." She was thinking, of course, of that famous voyage of Baudelaire's.

> *Mon enfant, ma soeur,*
> *Songe à la douceur*
> *D'aller là-bas . . .*

But the voyage of the play is not so different. It is a voyage many Americans made, intentionally or unintentionally, in the years between the two world wars when Pan Am's flying boats began to follow the sickle curve of the Antilles through the Leeward Islands and the Windwards.

What they meant to find — these later travelers — was a New World Capri or Antibes where they could build their houses off beyond the winter and play golf and bridge and meet for cocktails every evening. What they found was something altogether different — beauty of a kind they could not always bear: deep-water islands blazing with high veils of light and blowing with the northeast Trades — islands they knew they could not live in, could not leave.

It did not last long, that brief world of Far. After the Second World War its sky was webbed with the contrails of enormous jets and every cove had two hotels at least and you could telephone New York from anywhere. But for a few years, till that happened, men and women, playing at the living of their lives, sometimes almost found them in that wind, that moon.

A. MacL.

Silence.
the sound of the sea on a reef far out
the sound of a soft wind in palm trees
the sea on the reef
the wind in the palms
then suddenly a raucous record — rock-and-roll —
a door opens
the record drowns the sea sound and the wind

A WOMAN'S VOICE:
Chuck!
  Turn that *thing* off!
    Chuck!

(shriek of a needle across a record
silence
the sea sound
the soft wind)

THE WOMAN'S VOICE:
Oliver! Where are you?

OLIVER: (*British voice*)
    Here, Elizabeth.

ELIZABETH:
   I couldn't see you in the dark.

OLIVER:
   How suddenly it falls here!

ELIZABETH:
                              Yes.

OLIVER:
   And how the sea sound changes.

ELIZABETH:
                         Nearer?

OLIVER:
   Nearer and yet farther somehow.
   You remember where you are —
   an island.

ELIZABETH:
                    An island in the sea.

   (*the sea sound*)

   Chuck can't bear the island after dark.

   (*silence: the sea sound*)

   You heard him. Rock-and-roll.

OLIVER:
                         I heard him.

   (*silence*)

ELIZABETH:
   Where's Alice?

OLIVER:
                    Dressing I suppose.

172

A WOMAN'S VOICE: (*British*)
Dressed! Am I late, darling?

OLIVER:

Naturally!

ELIZABETH:
No. My island guests are. Always.

OLIVER:
Late? For dinner? It's impossible.

ALICE:
Now, Oliver. No more of that!

ELIZABETH:
At least we'll have the moonrise to ourselves:
It's brightening already. Look at it!

OLIVER:
And dinner?

ALICE:

Oliver! You're intolerable.

(*A door opens, closes.*)

Ah, there's Chuck.

CHUCK:

Right on time as
always, Alice. What will it be?
You, Oliver?

OLIVER:

Nothing. Nothing at all.

ALICE:
He's hungry.

CHUCK:

And they're late again.

173

I've known the whole American community
fifty minutes out by clock time.

OLIVER:
Extraordinary. Quite like natives.

ELIZABETH:
Not the least like.

CHUCK:
Fifty! Think of it.

ELIZABETH:
Not the least like natives, Oliver.
They have no word for time. They live
now.

OLIVER:
Only the trees have found that
fabulous country.

ELIZABETH:
The trees and I.

OLIVER:
On this island?

ELIZABETH:
On this island
here and now have met each other.

OLIVER:
The unattainable, unvisited now
that's never here when we are.

ELIZABETH:
No!
Now and here together in one gulp
to burn the heart out with its happiness.

174

CHUCK:
  Elizabeth!

ELIZABETH:
      I'm sorry.

OLIVER:
          Why be sorry?
  Only those who've been there know it.

ALICE:
  And most of them won't tell.

ELIZABETH:
              Sorry
  because I've never been there, then.

OLIVER:
  I wish your guests were now . . . *and* here.
  Are you quite sure you asked them, darling?

CHUCK:
  I'm sure!

OLIVER:
      Ah, it's Chuck that did it.

CHUCK:
  The Englishman and his stomach, Oliver!

OLIVER:
  Why shouldn't I be hungry? Lunch —
  Alice's and mine — was sandwiches
  seven thousand feet above
  the empty earth — and that was water.

ALICE:
  Cheese what's more.

OLIVER:

What's less!

ELIZABETH:

Look!
Look at the sky! It's brightening!

OLIVER:

For God's sake
don't divert me when I'm miserable.

CHUCK:
Watch these palm trees on the cliff now . . .

ALICE:
You're like a hen in thunder, Oliver,
brooding your addled eggs.

CHUCK:

. . . I planted them.
The moon, from where you're sitting, both of you,
rises — ought to rise — just there.
I worked it out myself with almanacs.
The February moon should rise
just in that frame of fronds precisely . . .
Some day this garden will be wonderful.
You wait! Another year. Two years.

ELIZABETH:
Why wait? Why not see it now?

OLIVER:
He can't. Nor you. Nor any of us.
Who was it said his whole life seemed
a preparation for what never happened?
Like your dinner, dear Elizabeth:
A preparation for who never comes.

ALICE:
How smooth the wind is. Like a river.

ELIZABETH:
The always flowing of the wind . . .

CHUCK:
They never fail, the Trades.

ALICE:
                              It feels —
the air against my face — as though
the air were still and the earth turning.

ELIZABETH:
I know. You feel the turning earth here.

ALICE:
Bodies should go naked in it.

OLIVER:
Not some that I can think of.

ALICE:
                              All!
All should go beautiful in Paradise!

OLIVER:
The Island Paradise! Who called it that?

CHUCK:
Columbus. On the second voyage.

OLIVER:
The Admiral was not precisely
reticent was he? I remember
one of his discoveries he called
La Desirada.

CHUCK:
La Désirade.
It's French now.

OLIVER:
And it takes the consequences?

ELIZABETH:
Quand bleuirat sur l'horizon la Désirade . . .

OLIVER:
What's that?

ELIZABETH:
Apollinaire I think:
"When will the desired land-fall
Loom — grow blue — on the horizon . . ."

OLIVER:
Another of Chuck's sort, Elizabeth —
Apollinaire. The sort for whom
no voyages ever come to shore
however the sad heart prepares for it.
That's the modern poet for you!
Journeys end in no one's meeting . . .
But Paradise! How did he know?

CHUCK:
Know what?

OLIVER:
The place was Paradise?

ALICE:
The Admiral?

OLIVER:
The Admiral.
How did he know? It must have looked
an island much like any island.

ALICE:
Maybe the Indians told him.

ELIZABETH:
                         They might have.
Those Arawaks were cheerful creatures,
pretty and gentle and so gay . . .

CHUCK:
Before the Caribs ate them and the Spaniards
relieved them of their sinful flesh
with whips and saltmines!

ELIZABETH:
                      Old philosophers
took them for witnesses of human innocence:
The primitive happiness of mankind.

CHUCK:
What Elizabeth means — the books latched onto them.
Rousseau's Noble Savage was an Arawak.

OLIVER:
Ah, that explains it all! Columbus,
seeing those laughing, splashing Indians
naked as jays and beautiful as children
knew at once what latitudes he sailed in.
The place was Paradise! That settled it!
Had he no eyes at all for reefs
or shark fins or the green volcanoes
lurking in this smile of trees?

ALICE:
They were the angels at the gate.

ELIZABETH: (*excitedly*)
I think he saw it all. And knew.
This was no island in the sea.

This was another kind of island —
a shoal in time where happiness was possible:
More perhaps than possible — inevitable.

OLIVER:
Inevitable? Happiness?

ELIZABETH:
                    Yes. Inevitable . . .
For those who found his island.

OLIVER:
                    Found it!
Thousands of wanderers must have found it —
Indians, Spaniards, Negroes, Frenchmen —
Even Americans! And were they happy?
Are they? All of them? Those Negroes
swinking half-naked in the cane?
Americans stark naked on the beaches?

ELIZABETH:
Few of them have found *his* island.

OLIVER:
Yes, and fewer ever will,
and fewer still return to tell of it.
Perhaps some bronze brown African woman
lying like summer in the sun,
languid with her mute desire,
might turn her head and be there — might!
But who else? Your American neighbors?
If one American should see this Paradise,
even from far off in his grog,
the way you think the Admiral saw it,
his mind would fail him! Don't deceive yourself.
We're all sleepwalkers here, Elizabeth.

You are. I am. Chuck there. Alice.
If we should find ourselves awake
where "now" was truly now, and "here"
just here, and nothing left to hide us,
we'd huddle shivering in our souls
like those who waken in cathedrals, naked.
Oh, we'd sweat I tell you. We'd be miserable.

ELIZABETH:
Some would. Some would laugh — or try to.
One or two would change their lives.

OLIVER:
Would they, Elizabeth? Change? You think so?

ELIZABETH:
Peter would go back to sleep.

ALICE:
Peter! Peter Bolt you mean?
Is he here? On this island? Peter?
Followed you all this way?

CHUCK:
                    Followed us!

ALICE:
Oh, not you, Chuck.

ELIZABETH:
                    Peter Bolt.
It's never now or here with Peter.
It's always somewhere else and afterward:
Afterward when the work is finished,
the fame won.

CHUCK:

        And you think that's strange?
You think, because I quit and came here
looking for — what you haven't found —
it isn't so with me too? All of us?

ALICE:

What is it that you haven't found? —

ELIZABETH:

What's all around us.

CHUCK:

             Is it? Is it?

OLIVER:

But this not quite impetuous Peter? . . .

CHUCK:

Lawyer. One of the best they tell me.
Young too. Must have heard his name.
He has a house here. God knows why:
He's never in it. One week. Two weeks.

OLIVER:

Here now?

CHUCK:

        They're dining with us.

OLIVER:

               They!

CHUCK:

He has a wife of course.

OLIVER:

         "Of course"?
That kind of wife? . . . Well? Isn't she?

182

ALICE:
Elizabeth is our authority.

ELIZABETH:
Authority?
Years ago I used to know him.
We haven't really talked for years.

CHUCK:
Ann, my love! Not Peter: *Ann*.

ELIZABETH:
No one can speak for Ann.

ALICE:
Not even
Ann.

OLIVER: (*to Alice*)
You know her?

ALICE:
Yes. She's beautiful.

ELIZABETH:
She's everything a woman should be.

ALICE:
There's nothing Ann can't do . . .

OLIVER:
But? . . .

ELIZABETH:
Feel.

ALICE:
Or know she feels at least.

183

ELIZABETH:

              Or show it.

OLIVER:

Patently, she's mad about him.

ALICE:

               Mad!
You haven't seen that smooth brown hair!

OLIVER:

And he? Does he deserve her?

ALICE:

             Dotes on her!
Thinks of her morning noon and night!
Where is she? Is she well? Safe? Comfortable?

ELIZABETH:

You think anxiety is proof of love?
It may be proof of love's disaster:
Duty doubling duty's care
because the passionate carefulness of the heart
no longer rushes breathless . . .

(*Oliver flings out of his chair, paces the gravel.*)

OLIVER:

             God!
I'm famishing. Where are these pretty people?
Do they exist? Or did Elizabeth
dream them in that elegant head
to populate her Paradise, her island?

ALICE:

Oh, they're real enough. I'd call
the J. B. Halseys real. Thick as
porterhouses, both of them.

184

CHUCK:

                    The Keoghs.

ALICE:
  Oliver wouldn't know the Keoghs:
  They're just simple, decent people!

CHUCK:
  From Milwaukee.

ALICE:

                  From Milwaukee.

OLIVER:
  They must be something more than simple.

CHUCK:
  Why?

OLIVER:
      To live here.

CHUCK:

                Why, to live here?

OLIVER:
  Live in this Paradise of Elizabeth's?

CHUCK:
  What's wrong with Paradise?

OLIVER:

                          For saints,
  nothing.

CHUCK:
          For simple, decent people.
  Even the decent have a right to happiness.

OLIVER:

Oh, a right! You Americans
guarantee it somewhere, don't you?
All men have a right to happiness —
you, the Keoghs, everybody.
What if happiness laid claim to them?
It might, in Paradise, you know —
people who all their lives have lived
pursuing happiness, pursuing something
more or farther off or brighter.
In Paradise there's nothing more.
Everything that will be, is.

ELIZABETH:

Is, and is everything!

OLIVER:

               They'd go mad.
We all would — all of us. We're all the same:
We live by what's still left to live for:
Something in another life,
another love, another country,
even in another world,
at least some other day. In Paradise
everything is here, is this:
The ordinary heart can't bear it.
Suffering, yes: suffering we endure.
But happiness! Happiness is long ago
or far away or not yet come to.
Only a child or those like children,
meeting happiness in a summer's door,
can take it by the hand and run with it.
The rest walk past it and remember.

ELIZABETH:

Some walk past it and forget.

OLIVER:

Your island, dear Elizabeth! Your island!
It's Shakespeare's parable all over.
Enchanting music draws us through the sea,
we glimpse an inexpressible happiness,
we turn into the things we were —
a duke, his daughter, attendants, gentlemen.

ALICE:

Oliver'd turn us into saints.

OLIVER:

Saints of a far more rigorous discipline
than any the meek church acknowledges.
Mexican Indians. Chinese poets.
No ordinary saint can sit
in sunlight at a door, like those
old Negro women of Elizabeth's.
Watch your compatriots at play or mine!
Look at the Riviera! Strewn with them!
The wreckage of the right to happiness
in painted shirts and canvas trousers
drinking Pernod before breakfast,
the possibility of Paradise so terrifies them!

ALICE:
And our compatriots here?

CHUCK:
                              They drink.
A little.

ALICE:
           Chuck!

CHUCK:
                  All right! They drink!
Why not? It passes time.

OLIVER:

> Does it?
> Not if the place is what he called it.
> Time in Paradise never passes.
> The blessed live their lives awake.

ELIZABETH:

> Each minute like the last that will be:
> Each like the first that ever was.

OLIVER:

> How wise the child is all at once.

ALICE:

> She's had her glimpses of the garden:
> Who hasn't?

OLIVER:

> Happiness is difficult.
> It takes a kind of courage most men
> never are masters of, a kind of
> innocent ruthlessness that lives
> like leaves in the instant of the air:
> The courage just to be — to trust
> the wind that blows you.

ELIZABETH:

> Look! The moon!
> It's rising!

OLIVER:

> Do you think that fact,
> Elizabeth, deserves remark
> just at this juncture of my discourse?

ALICE:

> How slow it lifts into the sky!
> Look at it, Oliver! It's marvelous.

OLIVER:
  Dear girl, we have a moon in England.

CHUCK:
  Only you never see it.

OLIVER:
                     Don't we!
  Demure among her clouds, not strutting
  naked like that tropical piece.
  Shameless the way she stares at us!

ELIZABETH:
                          They say
  the moon feeds on our eyes. I think
  I never saw a moon more gluttonous . . .
  I know I never saw one stranger:
  So still! Silver and intent and still!
  It burns like silence in a mirror.

CHUCK:
  Because the wind has fallen. Listen!
  The Trade Wind almost never falls
  night or day — not at this season.

ALICE:
  I hear a kind of murmuring in the sea —
  between the slidings of the sea a syllable.

ELIZABETH:
  So still! So still!

ALICE:
               I've never known
  the world — the sea, the sky, the air —
  so still.

ELIZABETH:
    Nor I.

ALICE:
            The palm leaves fill
    and fall as though not air but moonlight
    gathered them and let them go.
    You know, it could be Paradise, it could be —
    this moment anyway.

ELIZABETH:
                    It is!
    If only we ourselves awoke
    and trusted it, it could be. Even for
    us! If we could take it . . . Dared to . . .

CHUCK:
    Take what?

ELIZABETH:
            Our lives! Our lives! Our lives!

ALICE:
    Turn your face up! Close your eyes!
    Feel the almost imperceptible
    movement of cool and warm across your lids
    the moon makes touching you — the sliding moon.
    Something unimaginably beautiful
    seems no farther from me than my hand
    could reach, if I should lift one finger.

OLIVER:
    Alice is giddy from her fast.

ALICE:
    Jeer if you please. You feel it too.
    I know you, Oliver.

OLIVER:

    All right, I'm giddy.
Why not? If the moon is risen
it must be — God knows what it must be —
Ten?

CHUCK:

  It's half past eight.

OLIVER:

    Great God!
And not a sign of them. No message.
You don't suppose this settlement of yours
has vanished at the clap of moonlight?
Strange things happen in the wilderness.
Remember Raleigh's settlement at Jamestown?
Gone — just gone — the table set,
food in the kitchens, and the place
deserted. Not a soul. Perhaps
it wasn't Raleigh. Even Jamestown.

ELIZABETH:

Be quiet! Listen to the sky!

OLIVER:

Or those deserted ships at sea
discovered drifting with their sails set, everything
neat, everything in order — a child's
toy, the captain's toddy, biscuits —
even the cat's milk sweet and not
one single soul aboard — no explanation —
nothing but the slapping sails,
the groaning timbers . . .

ALICE:

    And the little girl
crunching popcorn in the row behind you!

CHUCK:

My guess would be they stopped at Peter's
meaning to have one drink and had
another and, just possibly, another.

OLIVER:

It isn't conceivable. I won't believe you.
People don't sit down and drink
while others hunger. No, they're gone.
Something — who knows what? — has tempted them
past the familiar safe stockade
to those dark forests off beyond it —
God have mercy on their souls! —
leaving the settlement uninhabited
save for ourselves: We few remaining.

ELIZABETH:

What makes you think we're safe inside,
we others? That blazing moon could burn
the whole stockade of certainty and leave us
ignorant in the wilderness, no matter
how we'd built it out of words from home.
Where would we hide our hunger then?

CHUCK:

Oh, for God's sake, no, Elizabeth.
I hate those games: You know I hate them.
Elizabeth is always asking:
Where? . . . When? . . .

OLIVER:

And you reply?

CHUCK:

That's it: I don't . . .

ALICE:
                    Listen! . . . Listen! . . .
    Chuck, there's something . . . not the sea . . .

CHUCK:
    It's them! They're coming!

OLIVER:
                        Ah, they're coming!
    How shall we welcome them, Elizabeth?
    Sit here as though we'd finished dinner,
    smoking our cigars, and rise,
    polite in our restrained astonishment,
    and wait until the boldest chirps:
    "It *was* tonight, dear, wasn't it?"
    And answer awfully: "It *was!*"?

ALICE:
    Oliver! He would! You know he would.
    Don't encourage him, Elizabeth.

OLIVER:
    You call that look encouragement?
    She hasn't heard a word I've said.

    (*wheels on gravel: hum of a car: the motor cuts: voices*)

CHUCK:
    Anything you want to bet
    they feel no pain.

OLIVER:
                    Those tell-tale voices!
    How hideously rum reveals
    the insipidity of its origins!
    Liquid sugar! Listen to them!

193

(The voices are louder: two men, one angry and the other laughing; two women, the first voice high and childish, the second self-consciously correct. Sound of a gate opening and closing.)

FIRST MAN:
God, boy, do I need a drink!

FIRST WOMAN:
What he means he needs another . . .

FIRST MAN:
OK!

FIRST WOMAN:
. . . little drink. He's beautiful!
The way he wears that shirt, he's beautiful!
Isn't he beautiful, Elizabeth?

FIRST MAN:
Boy, what I've been through!

FIRST WOMAN:
Just beautiful!

FIRST MAN:
Watching these goddam goofy idiots
gawk by the water while the moon
came up and gawked at them, for Chri'sake!

SECOND WOMAN:
Dear Elizabeth, forgive us!
We must be very, very late.
Peter's just behind. And Annie.

FIRST MAN:
Behind! He hasn't left that beach.
Poor bastard's stuck there staring at it
stiff as a jacked fish. Stiffer.

FIRST WOMAN:
                              Just
    Staring at it.

CHUCK:
                    Staring where?
    What's he staring at?

FIRST WOMAN:
                         Just staring.

SECOND WOMAN:
    Standing staring.

FIRST MAN:
                    Wouldn't let me
    speak not even.

FIRST WOMAN:
                    Imagine that!
    Not even Harry even speak!
    Each of us just stood there staring.

CHUCK:
    Where? At what?

FIRST MAN:
                    Beside the road there.

SECOND MAN:
    Where the road runs by the beach.

SECOND WOMAN:
    The moon. We watched it rising.

FIRST MAN:
                              She did!
    Stopped us all beside the dune.

SECOND WOMAN:
No one knows how long we stood there.

FIRST MAN:
I do. *I* know. Ask me darling.

SECOND WOMAN:
All of us had silver glasses.

CHUCK:
Glasses?

FIRST WOMAN:
Silver in the moon.
Peter gave us silver glasses.

FIRST MAN:
Keeps his cocktails in his car,
the thoughtful bastard.

SECOND WOMAN:
All of silver.
Oh, it was wonderful, Elizabeth.

ELIZABETH:
It sounds so. Do you know each other?
This is Alice Liam, Sally:
You know Alice, Sally, don't you?
Sally Keogh, Harry Keogh . . .
Oliver, do you know the Halseys?
This is Oliver Liam, Helen.
Mr. and Mrs. Keogh, Oliver.

KEOGH:
Colonel Keogh!

ELIZABETH:
Oh, I'm sorry.
Colonel Keogh.

196

KEOGH:

                Not at all . . .
Natural error. When the wars are ended
who remembers the poor soldiers?

HALSEY:

The poor soldiers seem to, Colonel.

SALLY:

Particularly colonels.

CHUCK:

                Oh
generals remember pretty well:
generals remember all the generals.

KEOGH:

You can go to Hell, the lot of you.

ELIZABETH:

Why did he stay there, Harry?

KEOGH:

                Who?

ELIZABETH:

Peter.

KEOGH:

        The beauty of the night!
Imagine that! At his age! Stuck there
staring at the island in the moon
as though he'd never seen it till that moment!

OLIVER:

Had he?

KEOGH:

        This is his seventh year!
It wasn't only Peter either.
Know what Halsey here was saying?

HALSEY:
  Forget it!

KEOGH:
            Don't you wish I would?
  Don't you? Halsey here was saying:
  "Yes!" Like that . . . "Yes!" . . . "Yes!" . . .
  Staring at the moon-rise: "Yes!" . . .

HELEN:
  It's true. I never saw him look so —
  not even at Hyannisport that summer.
  I don't know what he meant.

KEOGH:
                        Nor him:
  He doesn't either.

HALSEY:
            No! Forget it.

HELEN:
  I wish he'd looked at me like that:
  Just once.

SALLY:
        Like what?

HELEN:
              Oh, like a man . . .
  who sees the whole of his desire.

HALSEY:
  You don't know what you're saying, Helen.

HELEN:
  A man who saw his whole desire,
  near as the world was in that moon,
  might get it.

OLIVER:

    Yes. And where would he be?

ELIZABETH:

Here.

OLIVER:

    Or his desire?

ELIZABETH:

    Here.

KEOGH:

They're tight as mountain ticks, the lot of them.

SALLY:

They're crazy, everybody's crazy,
craziest night I ever saw,
like Paris, who was that was saying
Let's go crazy, dear, in Paris?
Who? We did too, we went crazy,
Just like Paris only rum,
I like rum, want to know what *I* did?
Want to know what little Sally
did?

KEOGH:

    Quiet! You're a big girl now:
You're forty-seven.

SALLY:

    I kept saying,
I'm beautiful! I'm beautiful!

KEOGH:

Shut up, I said. I meant it!

SALLY:
Oh,
I stood there naked by the water . . .
I mean . . .
I stood there . . .
(*silence*)

KEOGH:
What she means,
she's had one coke too many.

ELIZABETH:
Does she?
I think she means that she was beautiful!

SALLY:
Elizabeth, you flatterer!

ELIZABETH:
It isn't flattery.
Why are you frightened to remember?

SALLY:
I'm not!

ELIZABETH:
You are. You'd rather think
what Harry thinks — that you were drunk —
than know what you knew then.

SALLY:
Elizabeth!
I don't know what you mean.

ELIZABETH:
I think you
do . . . or did.
(*There is an awkward silence.*)

CHUCK:
            Let's go indoors:
The Bolts will be along. We'll have
that drink the Colonel needs indoors.

KEOGH:
  And how he needs it!

OLIVER:
                        Poor dear Alice,
  tottering for lack of food.

ALICE:
                        I thought
  you'd fainted, Oliver. I couldn't hear you.

SALLY:
  I want Elizabeth to answer me.
  Elizabeth has made me cry . . .
  I don't know why she did.

ELIZABETH:
                        It isn't
  You. It's all of us. We face our lives
  like young girls in a gallery of mirrors.
  Some glittering, unexpected moment
  shows us our images and we shriek
  with childish, hysterical laughter, caught
  naked in the simplicity of ourselves . . .
  You needn't stare at me. You know it — all of you.

HELEN:
  Dear Elizabeth! It's the island!
  People say things on an island —
  things they never meant to say:
  They feel so far off . . .

ELIZABETH:
                              Yes, and see
things they never meant to see
and tell themselves they've never seen them!
We shouldn't live here, any of us.
We're out of place in so much light!
The green volcano in those hills
could drown us in a flood of fire
and we'd go under giggling.

CHUCK:
                              Sweet
love! How violent you are!

ELIZABETH:
Go in. I'll follow you. Please go.
Forgive me.

CHUCK:
                Come and get it!

(*sound of the door opening*)

                              Ice
Cold! Coals of ice . . .

KEOGH: (*off*)
God that's good! What did he call it?

HALSEY: (*off*)
Coals of ice.

ALICE: (*off*)
                Elizabeth's volcano.

SALLY: (*off*)
Elizabeth's volcano!

CHUCK: (*off*)

Right! Where is she?

Elizabeth!

(*His voice is louder, as though calling from the open door.*)

Elizabeth!

HELEN:

Don't pester her.
Even hostesses must have their moments.

CHUCK:
What a woman of the world you are.

HELEN:
Your world, Chuck?

CHUCK:

And what a woman.
You smell like almonds. Only warmer.

HELEN:
Don't! Please don't! Oh, I know
it's nothing to us — either of us:
Just the usual salute. It isn't
that . . .

CHUCK:

What is it, then?

HELEN:

It's me:
I don't know who I am. I don't
know!

CHUCK:

You want a man should show you?

203

HELEN:
Please! I mean it Chuck. I heard
something that frightened me beside the water.
There wasn't any sound at all —
no sound at all and yet I heard
ravishing laughter on the sea
like negresses: In love they say
they shriek with laughter . . . it was horrible!
I stood there staring at the moon and heard
ravishing laughter on the water . . .
I don't know what I am, I don't know . . .

HALSEY: (*off*)
Pull the door shut, will you?

HELEN:

                     . . . anything.

HALSEY:
The Colonel hates the moon . . .

(*The door slams shut. Silence. A second car on the gravel. The gate opens.*)

ANN:
Peter, we're terribly late. Please come.

PETER:
You go. I need time . . . It takes
Time.

ANN:
       What does: What takes time?
I don't understand you, Peter.
What takes time? You've changed so.

PETER:

                         Have I?
I wish I knew I had.

ANN:

         Peter!
You don't — can't — mean that, Peter!

PETER:

Changed into something that can live.

ANN:

Where?

PETER:

       Here in this island — in this light.

ANN:

You couldn't bear it. Not this moonlight.
Not a night like this. I know you.
Oh, my dear, how well I know you.
You need to earn your life to live in it
even though the earning cost you
all your lifetime and yourself.
I know those obstinate hounds you ride to.
I hear them whimpering in your sleep
night after night.

PETER:

        For Christ's sake, Annie!
I said — if there were words to say it . . .

ANN:

Tell me. Try to tell me, Peter.

PETER:

I said that what I suddenly understood.
There in the moonlight, on the beach, was —
This is what it *is*! Just this! —
not something afterward or elsewhere.
You live it or you don't, but what you

live or don't live is just this:
This, this moment now, this moon now . . .
this man here on an island watching.
I understood it as you understand
a knife blade driven in your side:
The way you understand in dreams
that waken in a giddiness of certainty.

ANN:
   That passes when you waken.

PETER:
                          Yes!
   Yes! God, Annie, you're so sensible!

ANN:
   I saw the moon too, rising.

PETER:
                        You? . . .
   All my life I've lived tomorrow
waiting for my life to come:
Promises to come true tomorrow,
Journeys to begin tomorrow,
Mornings in the sun tomorrow,
Books read, words written,
All tomorrow. Cities visited.
Even this fever of the sleepless heart
slept away tomorrow . . . all of it.

ANN:
   Truth to be told at last . . . tomorrow.

PETER:
   We cling so to the skirts of suffering
like children to their mothers — hold

the hand that hurts our hand for fear
we'll lose ourselves unless it hurts us! —
Making a virtue of our cowardice:
Pretending that a sense of sin and shame
is holier than the happiness we fumble.

ANN:
What is it that you have to do?

PETER:
To do?

ANN:
What is it?

PETER:
I don't know.

ANN:
And so there is . . . is something, Peter?

PETER:
I need to know the thing I know.
I need to think a little.

ANN:
Yes.
I'll go. Come when you can.

PETER:
I promise.

ANN:
Promise! If we only could . . .

(*sound of the door opening; burst of voices*)

CHUCK: (*off*)
There they are!

SALLY: (*off*)

There *she* is!

KEOGH: (*off*)

Where's
Peter for the love of God?

ANN:

Coming.
He's coming. Do forgive us, Chuck . . .
Elizabeth . . . Where is she? . . . all of you.

(*the wind is rising; the door slams shut; a woman's footstep on the gravel*)

PETER:
Elizabeth!

ELIZABETH:

I didn't mean to startle you.
The rest of them went in. I couldn't.

PETER:
We're dreadfully late. It's all my fault.
I'm sorry.

ELIZABETH:

Don't be. Island chickens
cook forever without noticing:
All you need to do is baste them.
Island diners baste themselves.

PETER:
You heard?

ELIZABETH:

I couldn't help it.

PETER:

                    When the wind
fell and that sudden silence of the moon
touched everything . . .

ELIZABETH:

               With silver . . .

PETER:

                       Yes,
with silver . . . Where were you?

ELIZABETH:

                  Beneath
the palms there at the little table —
Alice and Oliver and Chuck and I.

PETER:
I was beside the beach road making drinks,
talking the usual idiotic nonsense —
nothing that would change a life . . . and
you?

ELIZABETH:
   As though I'd started out of sleep
and everything were possible.

PETER:

             I thought of
you.

ELIZABETH:
   And I . . .
        of you.

   (*silence*)

PETER:

We've known
too long in silence to find words.

ELIZABETH:

And so we've
found our silence.

PETER:

Why does it take so long to
learn? We tell our miserable
creeping hearts they were not made for happiness
and suddenly and all at once they're there.

ELIZABETH:
Happiness is real — the only
real reality that any of us
ever have glimpses of. The rest —
the hurt, the misery — all vanishes —
only the blinding instant left us . . .

(*a great gust of wind; the house door opens; the tangled
voices; Chuck shouting*)

CHUCK:
Soup's on! Soup's on!

KEOGH:
Dinner's over, supper's cookin'
Old Dan Tucker just stand there lookin'.

HELEN: (*speaking from the open door*)
Elizabeth was in the garden wasn't she?
There they are. There's Peter anyway.
Where's your Annie, Peter?

SALLY: (*from the door*)

Where's
Annie?

HELEN:
    Can't you hear us, Peter?

KEOGH: (*in the door*)
    Old Dan Tucker just stand there lookin'.

SALLY:
    The wind's up. He can't hear you.

HELEN: (*out in the garden now*)
                Peter!
    Where's your Annie?

PETER:
          She's in the house.

HELEN:
    She isn't, though.

SALLY:
         She's vanished — utterly.

OLIVER:
    A miracle, my friends, has happened:
    Dinner has been announced!

    (*silence*)

                  It may be,
    after such protracted misery,
    the word conveys no meaning. *Dinner!*

SALLY:
    Peter, they saw her on the cliff.

PETER:
    Cliff!

HELEN:
    She's not there now.

PETER:

What cliff?

SALLY:

Outside that window of Elizabeth's
where everything pitches off into the sea.
There's not five feet of level rock
between the window sill and . . .

KEOGH:

Listen!

What are you telling the poor guy!
Ann's all right. She always will be.

HALSEY:

Of all the women in God's world
Ann would be the last to . . .

SALLY:

What?

Go on and say it!

KEOGH:

You goddam girls!

You make my tooth ache where it shouldn't.
You're acting like a pair of mischievous,
wild, half-witted, crazy children
trying to terrify yourselves
by scaring all of us.

SALLY:

Drop dead!

And not from any cliff top either:
Just drop!

HALSEY:

Sally!

SALLY:
All right! —
"Sally!" What's got into everybody?
You know the cliff as well as I do.
There's one way out: it's through the room.

OLIVER:
She might have come and we not noticed.
Those coals of ice of Chuck's demand
the most meticulous concentration.

SALLY:
I leaned across the cliff's edge, looking.
There wasn't anything at all — not anything.
Only the moonlight on those black
enormous surges when they shattered:
They say they come from Africa, those surges.

KEOGH:
I swear to God I'll beat you, Sally.

(*sound of running feet: the door pulled shut*)

HELEN:
Peter doesn't believe you, gentlemen.

SALLY:
Some things you have to see yourself.

KEOGH:
Particularly things that haven't happened.

HELEN:
How can you know they haven't happened?

HALSEY:
Not by looking in the sea
for dead girl's bodies.

HELEN:
I think you're heartless,
both of you. Heartless! Heartless!

SALLY:
There's
Elizabeth. Behind you.

HELEN:
Where's
Ann, Elizabeth?

SALLY:
She's gone.

HELEN:
They saw her on the cliff outside your window.

HALSEY:
Be quiet! Will you be quiet, both of you??

SALLY:
Peter's gone to look for her.

ELIZABETH:
Out my
window!

KEOGH:
Yes. The whole thing's nonsense.
Peter knows the whole thing's nonsense.
There he is.

SALLY:
All right. Ask him.

PETER:
She's in the kitchen. Cooking.

OLIVER:

                Bless her!

PETER:
Something went wrong with the potatoes.

KEOGH:
There you have it, Sal, you idiot.

SALLY:
Kiss me!
        I forgive you, darling.

OLIVER:
Bless the woman! The potatoes.

*(Elizabeth has begun to laugh: a high, clear, sudden peal that
breaks off with a smothered sob.)*

HELEN:
Elizabeth!
        Nothing has happened.
                It's all right.

ELIZABETH:
Nothing. Nothing at all. Not anything.

(the sound of a cocktail shaker)

CHUCK:
Supper's over: breakfast's cooking.

OLIVER:
Shall we break bread?

ELIZABETH:

           At least there's bread . . .
and salt.

OLIVER:
And Ann's potatoes.

ELIZABETH:
Yes.
And Ann's potatoes.

(*silence*)

Are you coming, Peter?

(*We hear them go in. The door is pulled shut. The wind.*)

THE END